Discipleship in a Post-Christian Age

Discipleship in a Post-Christian Age

With a Little Help from C. S. Lewis

Thiago Silva

WIPF & STOCK · Eugene, Oregon

DISCIPLESHIP IN A POST-CHRISTIAN AGE
With a Little Help from C. S. Lewis

Copyright © 2025 Thiago Silva. All rights reserved. Except for brief quotations in critical publications or reviews, no part of this book may be reproduced in any manner without prior written permission from the publisher. Write: Permissions, Wipf and Stock Publishers, 199 W. 8th Ave., Suite 3, Eugene, OR 97401.

Wipf & Stock
An Imprint of Wipf and Stock Publishers
199 W. 8th Ave., Suite 3
Eugene, OR 97401

www.wipfandstock.com

PAPERBACK ISBN: 979-8-3852-4647-2
HARDCOVER ISBN: 979-8-3852-4648-9
EBOOK ISBN: 979-8-3852-4649-6

VERSION NUMBER 04/24/25

To my dear wife, Lidia.

Contents

Preface | ix

Chapter 1: Introduction | 1
Chapter 2: The Biblical Vision of Discipleship | 8
Chapter 3: The Cultural Context of C.S. Lewis | 35
Chapter 4: C.S. Lewis's Apologetic Method | 53
Chapter 5: A Discipleship Model for the Post-Christian World | 85
Chapter 6: Worship as the Goal of Discipleship | 107
Chapter 7: Bringing It All Together | 125

Bibliography | 133

Preface

Discipleship has always been countercultural. From the earliest days of the church, following Jesus has required more than mere intellectual assent or external morality—it has demanded a reorientation of the entire self around the truth of the gospel. Yet, in our modern world, where Christianity is no longer the assumed foundation of culture, the very concept of discipleship has been subtly reshaped. Rather than a lifelong journey of transformation, it is often reduced to a formula for self-improvement, an occasional religious experience, or a moral code detached from deep theological conviction.

This book was born out of a conviction that we need to recover a richer, more robust vision of discipleship—one that is biblically faithful, theologically grounded, and culturally aware. In an era dominated by expressive individualism, digital distractions, and radical autonomy, many believers have unknowingly embraced what sociologists call *Moralistic Therapeutic Deism* (MTD)—a shallow, feel-good spirituality that prioritizes personal happiness over holiness, affirmation over transformation, and a distant, uninvolved God over the sovereign Lord of Scripture. The effects of this drift are evident: biblical illiteracy is rising, church participation is declining, and many professing Christians struggle to articulate what makes their faith distinct from secular moralism. In short, we are experiencing a crisis in discipleship.

In these pages, I propose that one of the most profound guides for navigating this crisis is C. S. Lewis. While he wrote in a different time, his insights into reason, imagination, and community provide a much-needed framework for discipleship today. Lewis understood that faith is not merely about believing the right things but about being formed in a way that shapes our entire perception of reality. He recognized that people are not only convinced by rational arguments but are captivated by beauty and drawn into truth through deep, meaningful relationships. His works provide a theological, philosophical, and imaginative toolkit to help us reclaim a vision of discipleship that is intellectually rich, spiritually compelling, and deeply communal.

Throughout this book, I explore how the church can apply Lewis's threefold approach to counter the specific cultural challenges that threaten discipleship today. We will examine the modern crisis of identity, where gender, sexuality, and self-definition have replaced God's design as the foundation of human worth. We will look at the numbing effects of digital distraction, which erode our capacity for deep reflection, prayer, and spiritual formation. We will consider the loss of Christian community, where individualism has replaced covenantal belonging, leaving many believers isolated in their faith. And finally, we will see how all these trends culminate in a faith that demands nothing, transforms no one, and leaves the church ill-equipped to face the cultural moment.

But this is not a book of despair. It is a book of hope—a call to reclaim discipleship as a holistic, life-shaping pursuit that forms resilient, thoughtful, and deeply rooted believers. The path forward is not to retreat into fear or nostalgia but to recover the depth, wonder, and communal richness of Christian faith. With a little help from C. S. Lewis, we can rediscover a discipleship that is not only true but beautiful, not only doctrinal but imaginative, not only personal but profoundly communal.

I invite you on this journey—not merely as an academic exercise, but as an invitation to a deeper, richer life of following Christ. If we are to disciple the next generation in a post-Christian world, we must do so with minds awakened, hearts enraptured, and communities committed to living out the gospel together.

Dr. Thiago Silva
Lake Charles, Louisiana

Chapter 1

Introduction

CHRISTIANITY IN THE WEST stands at a crossroads. The cultural and social structures that once supported Christian belief and practice have eroded, leaving many believers feeling adrift in a rapidly changing world. In past generations, Christianity was the assumed worldview, reinforced by institutions such as schools, government, and even popular culture. Church attendance was a social norm, Christian moral values were widely accepted, and biblical literacy was relatively common, even among those who were not particularly devout.

Today, that foundation has crumbled. The rise of secularism, the dominance of individualism, and the increasing influence of relativism have reshaped the cultural landscape. In many cases, Christianity is no longer seen as a guiding moral force but as outdated—or even morally suspect. The public square often portrays Christian ethics as oppressive or regressive, and religious conviction is frequently dismissed as intellectually weak or socially divisive. Younger generations, raised in an era of digital connectivity and ideological fragmentation, now encounter competing worldviews more frequently than ever before. The assumptions that once made Christianity seem self-evidently true have faded, giving way to doubt, deconstruction, and detachment from organized religion.

This shift has led to a growing crisis of discipleship. Many Christians are unsure how to live faithfully and how to disciple others in a post-Christian world. The rise of the "nones"—those who identify with no religious tradition—signals that faith is not merely in decline; it is increasingly perceived as unnecessary or irrelevant. In response, churches face a pressing question: how do we disciple believers in an age that no longer assumes the truth, goodness, or necessity of Christianity?

Definition of Terms

Discipleship

Discipleship is the lifelong process of learning to follow Jesus Christ in thought, character, and action. It is not merely about acquiring theological knowledge or adhering to moral principles but about being transformed into the image of Christ through intentional formation. Biblical discipleship involves both instruction and imitation—learning from Christ's teachings while embodying his life and mission (Matt 28:19-20; Rom 12:2). It is relational at its core, as believers grow in faith through community, mentorship, and shared practices. Discipleship extends beyond personal devotion to holistic engagement with culture, equipping believers to live out their faith in every aspect of life. As Dallas Willard argues in *The Great Omission*, many contemporary churches have neglected the call to deep, transformative discipleship, reducing it to mere church attendance or doctrinal assent rather than an ongoing apprenticeship with Christ. True discipleship is not simply about learning what Jesus taught but becoming the kind of person who lives as he lived, reflecting the kingdom of God in daily life.[1]

Post-Christian Age

A post-Christian age refers to a cultural context in which Christianity no longer holds influence over society's values, institutions, and moral frameworks. Unlike previous eras where Christian beliefs shaped public life, ethics, and laws, the post-Christian world is marked by increasing secularism, religious pluralism, and skepticism toward religious authority. This shift does not mean that religion has disappeared, but that

---

1. Dallas Willard defines discipleship as "learning from Jesus to live my life as he would live my life if he were I," emphasizing that spiritual formation requires intentionality and daily practice (Willard, *The Divine Conspiracy*, 282-83). Dietrich Bonhoeffer underscores the costly nature of true discipleship, famously declaring that "when Christ calls a man, he bids him come and die" (Bonhoeffer, *The Cost of Discipleship*, 99), reminding us that grace is never cheap. Discipleship, therefore, is not an optional add-on to Christian faith but its very essence.

INTRODUCTION

Christianity is often viewed as outdated, irrelevant, or even oppressive in public discourse. Many in post-Christian cultures are not actively rejecting Christianity; they are simply indifferent to it. Mark Sayers, in *Disappearing Church*, argues that post-Christianity often retains the moral impulses of Christianity—such as justice and human dignity—but severs them from their theological foundations, creating a culture that seeks meaning without transcendence. In this context, the challenge of discipleship in a post-Christian age is not only to defend the faith but to present it in a way that rekindles spiritual longing and demonstrates its relevance in a world that has forgotten its need for God.[2]

The Crisis of Discipleship in a Post-Christian World

Three significant cultural forces make Christian formation particularly challenging today: secularism, relativism, and individualism. These are not merely external pressures; they have deeply influenced how Christians think, believe, and live. As a result, faith has become increasingly shallow, fragile, and easily swayed by cultural trends.

Secularism: Faith Without Depth

Secularism has marginalized religious belief, treating faith as a private and largely irrelevant aspect of life. Christianity, once embedded in the fabric of Western society, is now frequently viewed as outdated or oppressive. Many believers, shaped by this cultural shift, have compartmentalized their faith—acknowledging God in religious settings while granting him little authority over their daily lives, work, politics, or moral decisions. As a result, many Christians know fragments of the Bible but lack a coherent biblical worldview. Their faith cannot withstand intellectual challenges

---

2. Mark Sayers notes that post-Christian culture seeks the benefits of Christian values without submission to Christ himself (*Reappearing Church*, 2019). Charles Taylor, in *A Secular Age* (2007), explains how belief in God has shifted from being the default to just one contested option among many. Alister McGrath observes that the decline of atheism has not led to renewed faith but to spiritual confusion in a disenchanted world (*The Twilight of Atheism*, 2004). Aaron Renn describes our current moment as the "Negative World," where Christian morality often incurs social costs (*Life in the Negative World*, 2024). Carl Trueman traces how expressive individualism and the sexual revolution have redefined identity in ways that challenge traditional Christian beliefs (*The Rise and Triumph of the Modern Self*, 2020).

or moral pressures. Rather than confronting secular assumptions, many churches have conformed to them, reducing Christianity to therapeutic spirituality—offering practical life advice and personal encouragement rather than deep discipleship.

Relativism: Faith Without Conviction

Relativism has eroded the idea of objective truth, replacing it with personal preference and subjective experience. In today's culture, truth is often seen as fluid and adaptable, making moral absolutes seem oppressive or outdated. This mindset has seeped into the church, where many believers now pick and choose which aspects of Christianity to accept based on what feels right or aligns with cultural trends. Rather than submitting to the Bible as the authoritative word of God, many reinterpret or ignore passages that conflict with contemporary values. As a result, biblical teachings on sexuality, justice, and human identity are increasingly viewed as negotiable rather than non-negotiable.

Individualism: Faith Without Community

Western culture exalts personal autonomy as the highest good. The idea that each person must determine their own path in life, free from external authority or communal obligations, has deeply shaped the modern mindset—including how many approach Christianity. The church was designed to be a place of covenantal belonging, where believers grow together, challenge one another, and submit to the authority of Christ. Yet in a culture that prizes personal fulfillment above all else, commitment to a local church is increasingly seen as optional rather than essential. Many Christians now treat church as consumers—attending when it suits them but leaving when it demands too much. Without deep, committed relationships in the body of Christ, discipleship becomes an isolated, shallow endeavor that is easily abandoned in times of struggle or doubt.

The Consequence: A Church That Mirrors the Culture

The rise of what has been called *Moralistic Therapeutic Deism (MTD)* in the church is no accident—it is the natural result of a church that has absorbed cultural trends rather than resisted them.³ A faith influenced by secularism becomes shallow, treating Christianity as a private belief rather than a comprehensive worldview. A faith shaped by relativism becomes compromised, lacking clear moral and theological convictions. A faith influenced by individualism becomes disconnected, turning Christianity into a self-centered pursuit rather than a call to belong to the body of Christ.

The result is a fragile, rootless Christianity—one that struggles to endure hardship, cannot articulate its core beliefs, and ultimately fails to produce resilient disciples. Many abandon the faith not because they have carefully examined it and found it lacking, but because they were never truly discipled in it. They were given a feel-good version of Christianity that was incapable of answering life's deepest questions or sustaining them through suffering.

If the church continues down this path, it will not merely lose influence—it will lose its very identity. A church that mirrors the culture will always lose to the culture. The gospel was never meant to conform to the world's values; it was meant to confront, challenge, and transform them. And perhaps, the only way forward is to return to a discipleship model that is deeply biblical, spiritually rich, and culturally engaged, guided and empowered by the Holy Spirit. The church must recover its prophetic role—not by adapting to cultural trends but by standing firm in the unchanging truth of Scripture. If we fail to do this, we will continue producing nominal, disengaged Christians who, when tested, will walk away because their faith was never deeply rooted. This is why the insights of C. S. Lewis are so valuable.

Why C. S. Lewis?

C. S. Lewis offers a compelling vision of discipleship that speaks directly to the challenges of our time. He understood that faith must engage both the intellect and the imagination, shaping not only what we believe but how we see the world. His ability to integrate reason and beauty provides a model for Christian formation that goes beyond mere doctrine, awakening a deep desire for truth, goodness, and holiness. In an age where Christianity is often dismissed as either outdated or irrelevant, Lewis

---

3. *Moralistic Therapeutic Deism* (MTD) will be examined in more detail in Chapter 5, where we discuss the challenges of discipleship in a post-Christian world.

helps us recover a vision of faith that is intellectually robust, spiritually transformative, and deeply compelling.

He also anticipated many of the cultural forces that have weakened modern discipleship. He recognized the dangers of moral relativism, the erosion of objective truth, and the growing tendency to see faith as a matter of personal preference rather than divine authority. His insights into secularism, individualism, and the loss of meaning in modern life help diagnose why so many struggle with doubt, disengagement, and a shallow understanding of Christianity. His work provides believers with the clarity and confidence to navigate these challenges while remaining faithful to the gospel.

Lewis offers a way forward that is both timeless and relevant. His vision of discipleship forms believers who can think deeply, love truly, and live faithfully in a world that often resists biblical truth. By reclaiming a holistic approach—one that integrates reason, imagination, and community—we can cultivate a faith that is both steadfast and winsome, equipping disciples to stand firm and bear witness to Christ in an increasingly post-Christian culture.

Recovering Biblical Discipleship

This book will explore, with a little help from C. S. Lewis, how discipleship in a post-Christian age must integrate reason, imagination, and community—each playing a vital role in forming resilient followers of Christ. Reason ensures that faith is not based on blind belief but on truth that can be understood, defended, and lived out. Imagination shapes how we see the world, helping us not just to know the truth but to desire it. Community reminds us that discipleship is not an isolated pursuit but a shared journey within the body of Christ.

Discipleship in a post-Christian age is not about retreating in fear or lamenting what has been lost—it is about moving forward with confidence, courage, and conviction, trusting that the same gospel that transformed the world in the first century is still transforming lives today.

If the church is to reclaim a discipleship that is deep and transformative, we must begin by understanding what true biblical discipleship looks like. The crisis we face today is not simply the result of cultural shifts; it stems from a failure to grasp and embody the vision of discipleship that Jesus and the apostles set forth. Christianity was never meant to be a shallow,

INTRODUCTION

privatized belief system or a means of self-improvement—it is a call to wholehearted devotion, a lifelong journey of being conformed to Christ. Before we can address how to disciple believers in a post-Christian age, we must first return to Scripture to recover God's vision for discipleship. What does it mean to follow Christ? What does true discipleship require? And how did Jesus and the early church form disciples who could withstand cultural opposition and faithfully advance the kingdom of God? In the next chapter, we will explore the biblical foundation of discipleship, laying the groundwork for how we can recover and embody this vision today.

Chapter 2

The Biblical Vision of Discipleship

DISCIPLESHIP IS THE HEARTBEAT of the church's mission. Jesus' final command to his followers was a clear call to "make disciples of all nations" (Matt 28:19). This commission was not a suggestion for a select group of spiritual leaders but the central mandate for the entire church. Yet, discipleship is often misunderstood or narrowly defined in modern Christian life. In some churches, it is reduced to Bible studies or small groups. In others, it may be seen as primarily intellectual—learning doctrines and memorizing Scripture—while neglecting transformation of character, lifestyle, and mission.

To fully grasp the significance of discipleship, we must root our understanding in the entirety of Scripture. Discipleship is not an exclusively New Testament concept; it is present throughout the biblical story. From the calling of Abraham to the formation of the early church, God's plan has always involved shaping a people who reflect his character and participate in His mission. This chapter explores the biblical theology of discipleship, tracing its foundations in the Old Testament and its fulfillment in the New Testament through Jesus Christ and the apostolic church.

Discipleship in the Old Testament

Although the word "disciple" is not explicitly found in the Old Testament, the foundations of discipleship are deeply embedded in its narratives, laws, and prophetic writings. Discipleship in the Old Testament centers on the relationship between God and his covenant people. Through calls to obedience, faithfulness, and transformation, God shapes individuals and communities to reflect his character and participate in his redemptive mission. This vision of discipleship unfolds through God's call to Abraham, the giving of the Law, the leadership of key figures like Moses, and the prophetic hope for spiritual renewal.

God's Call to Abraham: The Beginning of a Covenant Relationship

The call of Abraham in Genesis 12:1-3 serves as the starting point for the biblical concept of discipleship. God's command for Abraham to leave his homeland is not merely an invitation to relocate; it is a radical summons to trust and obedience. Abraham is called to separate himself from his past identity, his security, and his familiar surroundings and embark on a journey with God, who promises to bless him and make him the father of a great nation through whom all nations will be blessed. In this divine call, we see the foundational themes of biblical discipleship: faith, mission, and formation—themes that will continue to unfold throughout Israel's history and ultimately culminate in Jesus Christ and his call to discipleship.

Abraham's story reveals that discipleship is fundamentally about trust in God. He is not given a detailed roadmap or a clear explanation of what lies ahead. Instead, he is called to follow God into an uncertain future, relying entirely on God's promises rather than his own understanding. His journey is filled with challenges, including times of doubt, fear, and failure, yet God remains faithful. Abraham's trust is tested in significant ways, such as when he and Sarah remain childless for decades, despite God's promise of descendants, and when famine leads him to seek refuge in Egypt. Each of these challenges serves as a refining process, shaping Abraham into a man of greater faith.

The pinnacle of Abraham's trust in God is demonstrated in Genesis 22, when he is asked to sacrifice his son, Isaac. This moment is not only a test of obedience but also of trusting in God's goodness and faithfulness, even when his commands seem incomprehensible. Abraham's willingness to obey—even when it meant giving up the very thing God had promised—reveals a heart fully surrendered to God's will. This episode foreshadows the sacrificial nature of discipleship in the New Testament, where Jesus calls his followers to deny themselves, take up their cross, and follow him (Matt

16:24). True discipleship demands absolute trust, even when the journey is difficult or when God's ways seem beyond human understanding.

Abraham's call is not for his own benefit alone. From the very beginning, God's purpose for Abraham is global in scope—"all the families of the earth shall be blessed" (Gen 12:3). This promise establishes a missional pattern that runs throughout Scripture: God calls and blesses his people so that they can be a blessing to others. Discipleship, therefore, is never merely a private spiritual journey; it is a calling to participate in God's redemptive plan for the world.

Abraham's descendants, the people of Israel, are later given a priestly role among the nations (Exod 19:5–6). They are to be a people who reflect God's glory, live according to his law, and bear witness to his righteousness. However, Israel often struggles to live up to this calling. Their failures underscore the need for a perfect disciple—Jesus Christ—who will embody and fulfill this mission completely. Jesus, as the true son of Abraham, ultimately brings the blessing of salvation to the nations through his life, death, and resurrection. His Great Commission to make disciples of all nations (Matt 28:19) echoes God's original promise to Abraham—that through God's people, the whole world will come to know him.

This theme of mission-driven discipleship continues in the New Testament Church. Just as Abraham was called to leave his homeland and go where God would send him, Jesus's disciples are called to go into all the world. The church is to be a community of faith shaped by God's promises, living out his mission to bring light to the nations.

Abraham's journey is not one of immediate perfection. His faith develops gradually, shaped by both his successes and his failures. Early in his journey, he struggles with fear and self-reliance, as seen when he deceives Pharaoh about Sarah in Egypt (Gen 12:10–20). Rather than trusting God's provision, he takes matters into his own hands, revealing his initial immaturity in faith.

Yet God does not abandon him in his weaknesses. Instead, the Lord patiently teaches, refines, and strengthens Abraham through each trial. Abraham's growth is evident when he intercedes for Sodom and Gomorrah (Gen 18), showing that he has developed a heart that aligns with God's justice and mercy. By the time we reach Genesis 22, we see a man whose trust in God is so deep that he is willing to offer his own son in obedience.

Discipleship is not about instant spiritual maturity; it is a lifelong process of growth and refinement. Just as Abraham was formed through experiences of both faithfulness and failure, so too are disciples today. God patiently works in his followers, using both their victories and their mistakes to shape them into people who trust him more fully.

Abraham's story sets the pattern for discipleship throughout Scripture. His life reveals that discipleship is a journey of trusting God, living on mission, and being continually formed by God's grace. Every believer today follows in this same path—called to trust God in uncertainty, to embrace the mission of making his name known, and to allow him to shape them through every experience of life.

The Covenant at Sinai and the Discipleship of a Nation

The story of Israel as a covenant people develops further at Mount Sinai, where God establishes his covenant with the nation after delivering them from slavery in Egypt. This moment is foundational in shaping Israel's identity and their calling as God's people. The giving of the Law (Torah) provides a comprehensive framework for discipleship, instructing them in how to live in faithful obedience to God. In Exod 19:4–6, God declares that Israel is to be his "treasured possession" and "a kingdom of priests and a holy nation." This identity is rooted in their relationship with God, who calls them to reflect his holiness through obedience to his commands. Unlike other nations that define themselves by cultural, political, or military power, Israel's distinction comes from their covenant with Yahweh. Their faithfulness to this covenant would not only determine their well-being as a people but also serve as a witness to the nations, demonstrating what it means to live under the authority of the one true God.

The Law is central to Israel's discipleship because it reveals how they are to live in covenant relationship with God. More than a set of rules, the Law is an expression of God's character and his desire for his people to walk in his ways. The Shema in Deuteronomy 6:4–9 is particularly significant in shaping the daily life of discipleship. Moses calls the people to love God with all their heart, soul, and might and to teach his commands diligently to their children. This passage emphasizes that discipleship is holistic, encompassing the entire person. It involves both internal transformation and outward obedience, integrating faith into every aspect of life. Israel's love for God is not meant to be compartmentalized; it is to be the defining feature of their existence, shaping how they think, speak, act, and relate to others. This holistic discipleship requires that faith be cultivated in the heart, impressed upon the next generation, and lived out in communal life.

Generational discipleship is also a vital aspect of the covenant. Parents are tasked with passing down the knowledge of God's word to their children, ensuring that each generation continues to walk in faithfulness. The commands to discuss God's word "when you sit in your house and when you walk by the way" indicate that discipleship is not confined to formal religious settings. Instead, it is woven into the rhythms of everyday life. Faith is not simply taught in structured settings like the synagogue, but it is also caught in daily interactions, conversations, and lived experiences. This principle of multi-generational discipleship is echoed throughout Scripture and remains essential for the church today. The Christian faith is not sustained by institutions alone, but by families and communities who intentionally pass it down through love, instruction, and example.

Moreover, the Law emphasizes justice, compassion, and community responsibility. Commands to care for the poor, protect the vulnerable, and maintain fairness in legal matters reflect God's desire for his people to embody his character. Discipleship is not limited to personal piety; it involves living out God's values in relationships and society. The Torah repeatedly calls Israel to remember their own experience as an oppressed people in Egypt, urging them to show kindness to the stranger, uphold justice for the widow and orphan, and ensure that economic practices reflect righteousness and mercy. Living in covenant with God is not just about worship or personal morality—it extends to how they conduct business, treat their neighbors, and care for the marginalized. By following the Law, Israel was meant to demonstrate to the surrounding nations what it looks like to live under the reign of a just and loving God. Their obedience was not simply for their own benefit, but for the sake of the world, revealing the wisdom, righteousness, and goodness of the Creator.

However, Israel's history is marked by repeated failures to uphold the covenant. The people often fall into idolatry, injustice, and disobedience. Despite these failures, God remains faithful to his promises, sending prophets to call Israel back to covenant loyalty. These prophetic calls highlight the importance of ongoing repentance and renewal in the discipleship process. The prophets remind Israel that discipleship is not about mere ritual or external observance but about a transformed heart that genuinely seeks God. They rebuke empty religious practices and call for a return to true justice, mercy, and faithfulness. Though Israel often strays, God's commitment to his people never wavers. Even in exile, he promises restoration, pointing forward to a new covenant where his law will be written on the hearts of his people.

This pattern of calling, instruction, failure, and renewal continues throughout Israel's history and ultimately finds fulfillment in Jesus Christ, who perfectly embodies the covenant and calls his followers into a new kind of discipleship. The Sinai covenant reveals that discipleship is not a static state but a dynamic journey of learning, growing, repenting, and re-committing. It requires perseverance, a heart attuned to God's voice, and a willingness to live counter-culturally in a world that often resists divine truth. The lessons of Sinai continue to resonate today, reminding the church that discipleship is not just about personal faith but about forming a people who reflect God's holiness and justice in every aspect of life.

The Role of Leadership and Mentorship in Old Testament Discipleship

Throughout the Old Testament, God raises up leaders to guide his people in discipleship. These leaders—prophets, priests, and kings—are tasked with teaching God's word, modeling faithful living, and calling the people to obedience. While some leaders succeed in this role, others fail, illustrating both the importance and the challenges of spiritual leadership. Leadership and mentorship in Old Testament discipleship reveal that faith formation does not happen in isolation but through relationships, guidance, and a commitment to passing down knowledge to future generations. The role of leaders is not merely to govern but to disciple the people in the ways of God, ensuring that his covenant remains at the center of their communal and individual lives.

Moses is one of the most significant figures in shaping Israel's discipleship. As the mediator of the covenant at Sinai, Moses functions as both teacher and mentor. He spends forty years guiding the Israelites through the wilderness, instructing them in God's ways and interceding on their behalf. His leadership is characterized by deep dependence on God, intercessory prayer, and tireless teaching of the Law. He does not simply provide rules for the people to follow but invites them into a relationship with God, calling them to love and obey him. Moses's mentorship of Joshua exemplifies the importance of raising up new leaders for the ongoing work of discipleship. Joshua serves alongside Moses for years, learning how to lead through direct experience and intimate instruction. Before his death, Moses commissions Joshua to lead the people into the Promised Land, encouraging him to meditate on God's word and remain strong and courageous. This transfer of leadership highlights that discipleship is not about personal greatness but about equipping the next generation to carry on God's mission.

The prophets also play a crucial role in discipleship by calling the people back to covenant faithfulness. Throughout Israel's history, the people repeatedly stray from God's commandments, falling into idolatry, injustice, and moral corruption. The prophets serve as God's messengers, reminding Israel of their covenant obligations and urging them to return to him. Prophets like Isaiah, Jeremiah, and Ezekiel emphasize that true discipleship is not merely about outward compliance with religious practices but requires a transformed heart. Jeremiah speaks of a future covenant in which God will write his law on the hearts of his people (Jeremiah 31:33), signaling a shift from external observance to inward devotion. Ezekiel echoes this vision, promising that God will give his people a new heart and put his Spirit within them (Ezek 36:26–27). These prophetic visions anticipate the work of the Holy Spirit in the New Testament, where inward transformation becomes a central aspect of discipleship. The prophets' role in discipleship is not only corrective but also hopeful, pointing to a future when God will fully restore his people and empower them to live faithfully.

The wisdom literature of the Old Testament also contributes to the theme of discipleship by emphasizing the importance of learning from wise mentors and living according to God's wisdom. The book of Proverbs frequently exhorts readers to seek wisdom and fear the Lord, framing wisdom as the foundation of a godly life. The wisdom tradition highlights that discipleship is not merely about following laws but about cultivating discernment, humility, and godly character. Parents and elders are portrayed as key figures in guiding younger generations toward righteousness. The relational nature of discipleship is evident in the repeated instruction to heed the voice of wise teachers, demonstrating that faith is transmitted through both instruction and example. In contrast to the prophets, who often call Israel to repentance, wisdom literature focuses on forming character before major failures occur. It presents discipleship as a lifelong pursuit of wisdom, in which individuals grow in their ability to navigate life in accordance with God's truth.

As Israel repeatedly fails to uphold the covenant, the prophets look forward to a time when God will bring about a new act of redemption. This hope centers on the coming of a Messiah and the outpouring of the Holy Spirit. Isaiah speaks of a servant who will bring justice to the nations and a time when "the earth shall be full of the knowledge of the Lord" (Isa 11:9). This messianic vision points to a future in which God's people will be fully transformed and empowered to live in obedience to him. The prophetic hope for spiritual renewal lays the foundation for New Testament discipleship. The promise of a new covenant, inward transformation, and the indwelling Spirit is fulfilled in Jesus Christ, whose life, death, and resurrection establish the means by which true discipleship takes place. Jesus's ministry builds upon the Old Testament vision of discipleship by calling his followers into a renewed relationship with God, one that is no longer mediated through the Law alone but through the transforming power of the Holy Spirit.

However, the Old Testament's emphasis on covenantal relationship, obedience, and communal formation continues to shape the church's understanding of discipleship. The role of leadership in discipleship is not obsolete; rather, it finds its fulfillment in the church's mission to make disciples of all nations. The wisdom of the prophets, priests, and kings serves as a reminder that spiritual leadership is a sacred calling—one that requires faithfulness, humility, and a commitment to passing on God's truth to the next generation. Just as Moses mentored Joshua, and the elders of Israel were charged with guiding the people, so too must modern-day discipleship involve mentorship, teaching, and relational investment. Through the lens of the Old Testament, it becomes clear that discipleship is not an individualistic endeavor but a communal and intergenerational mission, one in which leaders are called to guide others into deeper faithfulness to God.

The Old Testament lays a strong foundation for discipleship, revealing God's desire to shape a people who reflect his character and participate in his mission. Yet, as Israel's history shows, human efforts often fall short. The law, the prophets, and the wisdom tradition all pointed forward to a greater fulfillment—a perfect disciple who would embody God's covenant and establish a new model of discipleship. That fulfillment is found in Jesus Christ. In his life and ministry, we see the clearest and most complete expression of what it means to follow God fully.

Discipleship in the Life and Ministry of Jesus

The life and ministry of Jesus Christ represent the full embodiment and fulfillment of the discipleship vision revealed in the Old Testament. Jesus does not merely teach about discipleship—he lives it perfectly, both in his relationship with the Father and in his mission to redeem humanity. In him, the themes of trust, obedience, formation, and mission, which were introduced in the Old Testament, find their ultimate realization. As the true son of God, Jesus models what it means to live fully in submission to the Father's will, and he invites others to follow him on this journey. Through his teachings, actions, and relationships, Jesus calls people not simply to believe in him but to become like him, shaping their entire lives around the reality of the kingdom of God.

Jesus's call to discipleship is radical and holistic, touching every aspect of life—personal, relational, and spiritual. It is not an abstract or theoretical calling but a deeply practical and life-altering one. To be a disciple is to live under the reign of God, to be transformed by Christ's presence and teaching, and to participate in his mission to bring the good news of the kingdom to all people. Jesus does not merely provide intellectual instruction; he forms disciples through real-life experiences, showing them how to trust, obey, and live as citizens of God's kingdom.

Jesus's Call to Follow: The Invitation to Radical Commitment

The call to discipleship is a central theme in Jesus's ministry. In the gospels, Jesus repeatedly invites people to "follow me"—a phrase that demands a response and implies total life transformation. This call is not merely a request for companionship or intellectual agreement but an invitation to radical obedience, surrender, and formation into christlikeness.

In Matthew 4:18–22, Jesus calls Peter, Andrew, James, and John while they are fishing, saying, "Follow me, and I will make you fishers of men." Immediately, they leave their nets and follow him, symbolizing the totality of the commitment Jesus requires. Their immediate response reflects the decisive nature of true discipleship. Jesus does not invite them to follow at their convenience, nor does he allow them to bring their old lives with them. They abandon livelihood, security, and family ties to embrace a new identity as his disciples.

THE BIBLICAL VISION OF DISCIPLESHIP

Jesus's call is both personal and authoritative. He does not provide a detailed roadmap or assurances of comfort and success but simply asks for trust. Discipleship begins with surrender—a willingness to leave behind one's former life to embark on a journey with Jesus as Lord and Teacher. This radical call echoes God's command to Abraham to leave his homeland and trust in his promises. However, in Jesus, the call is even more demanding, as it is a call to follow the very son of God in complete devotion.

Throughout his ministry, Jesus challenges potential disciples to count the cost of following him. In Luke 9:23, He declares, "If anyone would come after me, let him deny himself and take up his cross daily and follow me." This statement emphasizes that discipleship involves self-denial, sacrifice, and daily commitment to obedience. The cross, a symbol of suffering and death, represents the ultimate cost of discipleship. To follow Jesus means to surrender personal ambitions, comfort, and security in order to embrace the higher calling of God's kingdom. This is reinforced in Luke 14:26-33, where Jesus demands that his followers place their allegiance to him above all else, including family, wealth, and personal desires.

Jesus's radical call exposes the half-hearted nature of many would-be disciples. Some, like the rich young ruler (Mark 10:17-22), are eager to follow but unwilling to let go of their attachments. Others make excuses, postponing their commitment to Christ (Luke 9:57-62). These encounters reveal that discipleship is not a casual affiliation—it is an all-encompassing call to reorder one's life around Jesus.

At the same time, Jesus's call to follow is not merely about sacrifice—it is an invitation to abundant life. He does not call his disciples into despair but into a deeper experience of joy, purpose, and intimacy with God. In John 10:10, Jesus declares, "I came that they may have life and have it abundantly." This statement reframes discipleship as a journey not of loss, but of gain. Those who leave behind earthly security gain something far greater—life in communion with God.

The paradox of discipleship is that through self-denial and surrender, one finds true life and freedom in Christ. Jesus assures his disciples that even when they suffer, they are never abandoned. He promises them rest for their souls (Matt 11:28-30), the Father's provision (Matt 6:25-34), and the gift of eternal life (John 3:16). This reality transforms discipleship from a burdensome duty into a joyous privilege.

As Jesus calls his followers into radical commitment, he also forms them through relationship. Discipleship is not merely about learning principles or doctrines but about walking with Jesus, observing his life, and being shaped by his presence. Unlike the religious leaders of his day, who kept their followers at a distance, Jesus lives among his disciples, sharing meals, traveling, and engaging in real-life situations with them. His discipleship method is intensely relational—He teaches through example, conversation, and direct experience, forming their character as much as their understanding.

The call to follow Jesus is not just about leaving something behind—it is about being transformed into something new. Those who follow Jesus are not simply admirers of his teachings; they are apprentices in his way of life. They learn to see as he sees, love as he loves, and serve as he serves. They are invited not merely to listen to sermons but to participate in the very work of the kingdom.

Through his teaching, his relational mentoring, his use of imagination and parables, and his emphasis on mission, Jesus redefines discipleship. It is not a program, a theory, or an individual pursuit—it is a lifelong, transformative journey of becoming more like him.

As we continue exploring Jesus's model of discipleship, we will see that his training of the twelve, his use of parables and imagination, and his emphasis on love, service, and sacrifice all work together to form a community of disciples who will one day carry his mission to the ends of the earth. Discipleship in Jesus's ministry is not about personal enlightenment—it is about preparing people to live for God's glory and bring his kingdom into the world.

Relational Discipleship: Jesus's Method of Mentorship

Jesus's approach to discipleship is profoundly relational. Unlike the religious leaders of His time, who maintained a hierarchical distance from their followers, Jesus lives alongside his disciples, investing deeply in them. He does not merely deliver abstract teachings to large crowds—though he often preaches publicly—but he walks with, eats with, and personally instructs a small group of men, shaping their character through constant interaction, shared experiences, and practical training. This relational model mirrors mentorship structures found in the Old Testament, particularly in the relationships between Moses and Joshua, Elijah and Elisha, and the family-based discipleship seen in the wisdom tradition.

THE BIBLICAL VISION OF DISCIPLESHIP

The gospels highlight the central role of the twelve apostles in Jesus's ministry. These men are chosen not because of their social status, education, or religious training, but simply because of Jesus's sovereign call. They come from diverse backgrounds—fishermen (Peter, James, John, and Andrew), a tax collector (Matthew), and a political zealot (Simon). By calling this diverse group, Jesus demonstrates that discipleship is not restricted to a particular social class or occupation; it is open to all who are willing to follow him in faith and obedience. This challenges the conventional wisdom of the time, where religious instruction was typically reserved for elite students trained under esteemed rabbis. Instead, Jesus chooses ordinary men and transforms them into extraordinary leaders, equipping them to carry out his mission.

Jesus's relational discipleship is characterized by both proximity and intentionality. He does not simply impart knowledge; he immerses his disciples in a shared life, allowing them to witness his example up close. He invites them to live with him, observe his actions, and participate in his ministry. This is evident in moments where he allows them to witness his compassion toward the broken, his power over nature and demons, and his wisdom in answering difficult questions. He frequently pulls them aside for deeper instruction and personal correction, reinforcing what they have seen and heard.

One clear example of this pattern is found in Mark 4:10–20, where, after teaching the parable of the sower to the crowds, Jesus takes his disciples aside and explains its meaning privately. This deliberate action underscores that discipleship is not merely about hearing sermons but about internalizing spiritual truths through careful instruction and reflection. Similarly, when Jesus walks on water in Matthew 14:22–33, he does not merely perform a miracle for the sake of spectacle. Instead, he invites Peter to step out in faith, using the moment as a personal lesson on trust and dependence on God. Through these interactions, Jesus teaches his disciples not only what to believe but how to live by faith.

This close relationship allows Jesus to model what it means to live under the reign of God. He does not just tell his disciples to love their enemies; he prays for those who persecute him. He does not merely teach about servanthood; he washes his disciples' feet (John 13:1–17), showing that true leadership is rooted in humility and self-sacrifice. He does not only command his disciples to trust the Father; he demonstrates perfect trust, even in his deepest suffering in Gethsemane, where he prays, "Not my will, but yours be done" (Luke 22:42). Every aspect of Jesus's life serves as a living lesson in discipleship, showing his followers what faithful obedience to the Father looks like in real life.

Jesus's disciples do not simply learn his teachings—they imitate his character and actions. This method of relational discipleship prepares them not only to be transformed themselves but also to go and make disciples of others. In Luke 10, Jesus sends out seventy-two of his followers to preach, heal, and proclaim the kingdom of God, reinforcing the idea that discipleship is not passive learning but active participation in God's work. After their mission, Jesus debriefs with them, celebrating their victories while correcting their misunderstandings (Luke 10:17–20).

This model of mentorship shapes the entire future of Christian discipleship. The apostles, having learned directly from Jesus, continue this relational model in the early church. Paul, for example, disciples Timothy and Titus in the same way, investing in their lives and entrusting them with the responsibility of leading others (2 Tim 2:2). The principle remains the same: Discipleship is not about information transfer alone—it is about life-on-life transformation.

Jesus's approach to discipleship stands in contrast to modern models that sometimes emphasize programs over relationships, knowledge over transformation, and attendance over genuine spiritual growth. His method calls the church back to a deeply personal, intentional, and relational approach to forming disciples—one that moves beyond lectures and studies to shared life, deep accountability, and hands-on mission. His life demonstrates that discipleship is not simply about knowing Jesus's teachings but becoming like him.

By investing deeply in a few, Jesus ensures that his mission will continue long after his earthly ministry is complete. He does not seek quick numerical growth but depth and faithfulness, knowing that fully trained disciples will go on to make more disciples. This is the foundation of true, biblical discipleship—a commitment to walking alongside others, modeling christlike living, and equipping the next generation to follow him faithfully.

Teaching Through Parables and Imagination

One of Jesus's most distinctive teaching methods is his use of parables—short, imaginative stories that convey spiritual truths. Parables engage both the mind and the heart, inviting listeners to reflect deeply on the nature of

God, the kingdom of heaven, and the human condition. Jesus uses familiar images from everyday life—seeds, farmers, shepherds, and banquets—to illustrate profound theological concepts.

In Matthew 13, Jesus explains that he uses parables to reveal the mysteries of the kingdom of heaven to those who are spiritually receptive while concealing these truths from those who are hardened in unbelief. This dual purpose highlights the importance of both openness and discernment in discipleship. Disciples must cultivate a heart that is attentive to God's word and willing to be transformed by it.

Parables often challenge conventional thinking and provoke a response. For example, the parable of the good samaritan (Luke 10:25-37) confronts cultural prejudices by portraying a Samaritan—a member of a despised ethnic group—as the hero who exemplifies neighborly love. The parable of the prodigal son (Luke 15:11-32) reveals the extravagant grace of the Father, challenging both rebellious sinners and self-righteous individuals to repent and receive God's mercy.

By using stories, Jesus appeals to the imagination, helping his disciples see the world through the lens of God's kingdom. This imaginative engagement is essential for discipleship because it shapes how people perceive reality. Disciples are called not only to understand theological truths intellectually but also to embody them in their lives, allowing God's kingdom values to reshape their priorities, relationships, and actions.

Transformation and Obedience: Becoming Like Jesus

A key aspect of discipleship in Jesus's ministry is personal transformation. Jesus does not merely call his followers to assent to a set of beliefs; he calls them to become new people who reflect his character. This transformation is made possible through the renewing work of the Holy Spirit, which Jesus promises to his disciples. In John 14:16-17, he assures them that the Spirit will dwell within them, guiding them into all truth and empowering them to live in obedience.

Transformation in discipleship involves both inward renewal and outward obedience. Jesus emphasizes that true discipleship is marked by obedience to his commands. In John 14:15, he says, "If you love me, you will keep my commandments." Obedience flows from a relationship of love and trust. It is not motivated by fear or legalism but by a desire to honor the One who has redeemed and called us.

The Beatitudes in the sermon on the Mount (Matt 5:1–12) provide a vision of the character that Jesus seeks to form in his disciples. Traits such as humility, mercy, purity of heart, and peacemaking reflect the values of God's kingdom. Jesus contrasts these values with the self-centered priorities of the world, calling his disciples to be "salt and light" in a dark and decaying world (Matt 5:13–16).

However, transformation is not instantaneous. The disciples often struggle to understand Jesus's teachings and fail to live up to his expectations. Peter, for example, denies Jesus three times during his trial, despite his earlier bold declaration of loyalty (Matt 26:69–75). Yet Jesus does not abandon his disciples in their failures. After his resurrection, he restores Peter and commissions him to shepherd his flock (John 21:15–19). This act of grace underscores that discipleship is a process of ongoing growth, repentance, and restoration.

The Mission of Discipleship: Making Disciples of All Nations

Jesus's ministry of discipleship reaches its climax in the Great Commission, recorded in Matthew 28:18–20. After his resurrection, Jesus appears to his disciples and declares, "All authority in heaven and on earth has been given to me. Go therefore and make disciples of all nations, baptizing them in the name of the Father and of the Son and of the Holy Spirit, teaching them to observe all that I have commanded you." This command marks the transition from Jesus's personal ministry to the global mission of the church, ensuring that the work of discipleship will continue beyond his earthly presence.

This commission expands the scope of discipleship far beyond its earlier context. No longer is discipleship limited to those who physically walked with Jesus—now, his followers are commissioned to spread the message of the gospel to all people, across every nation, culture, and generation. This shift reveals the universal nature of Christ's mission, demonstrating that the kingdom of God is not bound by ethnicity, geography, or social status. The call to make disciples of all nations reflects God's original promise to Abraham in Genesis 12:3, that through Abraham's descendants, "all the families of the earth shall be blessed." The Great Commission is the fulfillment of that promise, with Christ's disciples serving as the agents of God's redemptive plan for the world.

THE BIBLICAL VISION OF DISCIPLESHIP

The command to make disciples is not simply about converting people to Christianity but about forming them into lifelong followers of Jesus. This process involves both evangelism and teaching, as seen in the two actions that follow: baptizing and teaching. Baptism signifies entry into the community of faith, marking a new believer's identification with Christ's death, burial, and resurrection. Teaching ensures that discipleship is not merely a one-time decision but an ongoing process of transformation and obedience. Jesus does not commission his followers to simply make converts—he calls them to raise up disciples who will walk in his ways, obey his commands, and teach others to do the same.

The success of this mission does not rest solely on human effort but depends on the power and presence of the Holy Spirit. In Acts 1:8, Jesus reassures his disciples, saying, "You will receive power when the Holy Spirit has come upon you, and you will be my witnesses in Jerusalem and in all Judea and Samaria, and to the end of the earth." The Spirit is the divine enabler of discipleship, equipping believers with wisdom, boldness, and spiritual gifts to carry out Christ's mission. Without the Spirit, the disciples would have lacked the courage and ability to fulfill their calling. But through the Spirit, they become bold proclaimers of the gospel, turning the world upside down with the message of Christ.

The book of Acts provides a vivid picture of the early church embodying this mission. The apostles proclaim the gospel in Jerusalem, Judea, and beyond, forming communities where believers devote themselves to teaching, fellowship, prayer, and breaking of bread (Acts 2:42). Through persecution, miracles, and divine guidance, the gospel spreads to gentile nations, fulfilling Jesus's command to make disciples of all nations. The church does not grow merely through strategic planning or human effort but through the sovereign work of the Spirit, guiding and empowering each step of the mission.

In the life and ministry of Jesus, we see the perfect model of discipleship. He calls people to follow him with radical commitment, teaching them through both words and actions. He invests in relational mentorship, walking closely with his disciples, correcting, encouraging, and equipping them for future leadership. He teaches through imagination and parables, using stories and metaphors to reveal deep spiritual truths. He emphasizes personal transformation and obedience, calling his followers not only to believe in him but to live in full alignment with God's will. And finally, he commissions his disciples to continue his mission, entrusting them with the responsibility of spreading the gospel and making disciples across the world.

Discipleship is not a static event but a dynamic and ongoing process. It is the process of becoming like Jesus, growing in faith, deepening in obedience, and participating in his redemptive work. It does not end with conversion but continues throughout one's entire life, as believers are continually formed into the image of Christ. The mission of discipleship is not merely an optional activity for certain Christians—it is the central calling of every believer. Jesus's final command is a commission to all who follow him, making it clear that discipleship is not just for pastors, missionaries, or church leaders, but for every person who confesses Christ as Lord.

The Great Commission remains as relevant today as it was when Jesus first spoke it. The church is still called to make disciples, to teach the truth of Christ, and to equip believers to live as faithful witnesses of his kingdom. Every Christian is part of this unfolding story of discipleship, carrying forward the mission that began with Jesus and continues through the power of the Holy Spirit. As we follow Christ, we are not only being transformed into his likeness, but we are also invited to take part in the greatest mission in history—the expansion of God's kingdom to every nation, tribe, and tongue.

Jesus did not merely call individuals to follow him; he trained them to carry on his mission after his departure. The Great Commission was not an abstract command but a continuation of his relational, intentional approach to discipleship. As the early church emerged, the apostles faced the challenge of forming new believers into mature disciples, navigating persecution, and spreading the gospel across diverse cultures. How did they carry out this calling, and what can we learn from their model?

Discipleship in the Early Church

After the resurrection and ascension of Jesus, the task of discipleship was entrusted to his followers. Through the empowerment of the Holy Spirit at Pentecost, the early church began its mission to make disciples of all nations, fulfilling the Great Commission (Matt 28:18–20). The early church's understanding of discipleship was shaped by the teachings and example of Jesus, as well as by the ongoing presence of the Holy Spirit. Discipleship became both the means and the goal of the church's mission, involving the formation of communities where believers grew in faith, character, and obedience.

THE BIBLICAL VISION OF DISCIPLESHIP

The Apostles and Their Role in Discipleship

The apostles played a central role in the discipleship efforts of the early church. As those who had walked with Jesus and witnessed his resurrection, they were uniquely positioned to continue his ministry. In Acts 1:8, Jesus promised his disciples, "You will receive power when the Holy Spirit has come upon you, and you will be my witnesses in Jerusalem and in all Judea and Samaria, and to the end of the earth." The apostles were to bear witness to Jesus's life, death, and resurrection, inviting others to become his disciples.

Peter's sermon at Pentecost (Acts 2:14–41) marked the beginning of the church's public ministry. Filled with the Holy Spirit, Peter boldly proclaimed the gospel, emphasizing that Jesus was both Lord and Christ. His message led to the conversion of about 3,000 people, who were baptized and joined the fledgling Christian community. This event illustrates the central role of proclamation in the early church's discipleship strategy. Discipleship begins with an encounter with the gospel, which calls people to repentance, faith, and a new identity in Christ.

The apostles' authority was rooted in their personal relationship with Jesus and their role as eyewitnesses of his resurrection. However, their leadership in discipleship was not authoritarian. Instead, they modeled humility, service, and reliance on the Holy Spirit. In 1 Peter 5:1–3, Peter exhorts church leaders to "shepherd the flock of God that is among you" with gentleness and as examples, not by "domineering over those in [their] charge." This servant leadership reflects the example of Jesus, who taught that greatness in his kingdom is measured by one's willingness to serve (Mark 10:43–45).

The apostles also emphasized the importance of multiplying discipleship efforts through mentorship and delegation. Paul, for example, trained and mentored leaders such as Timothy and Titus, entrusting them with the responsibility of teaching and guiding others. In 2 Timothy 2:2, Paul writes, "What you have heard from me in the presence of many witnesses entrust to faithful men, who will be able to teach others also." This generational approach to discipleship ensured the continued growth and health of the church.

The Empowering Presence of the Holy Spirit

A defining feature of discipleship in the early church was the empowerment of the Holy Spirit. Jesus had promised that the Spirit would guide his disciples into all truth and empower them to carry out his mission (John 14:16–17; Acts 1:8). This promise was fulfilled at Pentecost, when the Holy Spirit descended upon the gathered disciples, enabling them to speak in various languages and proclaim the gospel with boldness (Acts 2:1–13).

The Holy Spirit played several crucial roles in the process of discipleship. First, the Spirit provided the power and courage needed to witness to the gospel. Prior to Pentecost, the disciples were often fearful and uncertain about their mission. However, after receiving the Spirit, they became bold proclaimers of the faith, even in the face of persecution. Peter, who had previously denied Jesus, stood before thousands at Pentecost and later defied the Sanhedrin's orders to stop preaching (Acts 4:18–20).

Second, the Spirit was the source of spiritual transformation. The early church recognized that discipleship involved not only learning doctrines but also being transformed into the likeness of Christ. Paul emphasizes this process in 2 Corinthians 3:18, stating that believers "are being transformed into [the Lord's] image with ever-increasing glory, which comes from the Lord, who is the Spirit." The Spirit works in disciples to produce the fruit of the Spirit—qualities such as love, joy, peace, and self-control (Gal 5:22–23).

Third, the Spirit provided wisdom and guidance for the church's mission. In Acts 13:2–3, the Holy Spirit directs the church in Antioch to set apart Paul and Barnabas for missionary work. Throughout the book of Acts, we see the Spirit leading the disciples to new opportunities for ministry, confirming their decisions, and empowering their efforts.

The presence of the Spirit also fostered unity within the church. Despite the diversity of backgrounds among early Christians—Jews, gentiles, rich, poor, free, and enslaved—the Spirit created a bond of fellowship that transcended these divisions. In Ephesians 4:3–4, Paul urges believers to "make every effort to keep the unity of the Spirit through the bond of peace," emphasizing that there is "one body and one Spirit."

The Formation of Christian Community

Discipleship in the early church was not an individualistic endeavor but a communal one. New believers were incorporated into the church, where they experienced fellowship, worship, and mutual support. Acts 2:42–47 provides a vivid description of the early Christian community: "They devoted themselves to the apostles' teaching and to fellowship, to the breaking of bread and to prayer. Everyone was filled with awe at the many wonders and signs performed by the apostles. All the believers were together and had everything in common. They sold property and possessions to give to anyone who had need."

This passage highlights several key practices of discipleship within the early church. The believers devoted themselves to the apostles' teaching, indicating a commitment to ongoing instruction in the faith. This teaching likely included both the message of the gospel and ethical guidance on how to live as followers of Christ.

Fellowship was another essential aspect of discipleship. The Greek word for fellowship, *koinonia*, implies deep relational sharing and participation in one another's lives. The early Christians shared their resources to meet one another's needs, demonstrating sacrificial love and generosity. This communal life was a powerful witness to the surrounding society, as people saw the transformative impact of the gospel on human relationships.

Worship and prayer were also central to the life of the early church. The breaking of bread, which likely refers to both shared meals and the celebration of the Lord's Supper, reinforced the disciples' unity in Christ. Prayer sustained the church in times of both joy and persecution, as believers sought God's guidance and strength.

The early Christian community was marked by both growth and vulnerability. As the church expanded, it faced internal challenges, such as the neglect of certain widows in the daily distribution of food (Acts 6:1). The apostles responded by appointing deacons to oversee this task, ensuring that the church's ministries were carried out effectively. This example underscores the importance of leadership development and the delegation of responsibilities in discipleship.

Teaching and Spiritual Growth

The teaching of the apostles formed the foundation of discipleship in the early church. Their message was centered on the person and work of Jesus Christ, whom they proclaimed as the fulfillment of God's promises in the Old Testament. Through both public preaching and private instruction, the apostles sought to ground new believers in the truth of the gospel.

Paul's letters provide rich insight into the content and method of early Christian teaching. In his epistles to various churches, Paul addresses theological issues, offers practical exhortations, and encourages believers to persevere in their faith. For example, in Ephesians 4:11–16, Paul emphasizes the goal of discipleship as spiritual maturity: "So Christ himself gave the apostles, the prophets, the evangelists, the pastors and teachers, to equip his people for works of service, so that the body of Christ may be built up until we all reach unity in the faith and in the knowledge of the Son of God and become mature, attaining to the whole measure of the fullness of Christ."

Paul stresses that discipleship involves both knowledge and action. Believers are to be equipped for works of service, contributing to the growth and health of the entire body of Christ. Spiritual maturity is not an individual achievement but a communal process in which all members of the church support and encourage one another.

Mentorship played a vital role in early Christian discipleship. Leaders like Paul, Barnabas, and Priscilla and Aquila invested in younger disciples, training them to carry on the work of ministry. Timothy, for example, was mentored by Paul and entrusted with leadership responsibilities in the church at Ephesus. Paul's letters to Timothy provide both personal encouragement and practical guidance for his role as a pastor and teacher.

The Mission to Spread the Gospel

The early church understood discipleship as inherently missional. The command to make disciples of all nations drove the church's efforts to evangelize, plant churches, and train leaders. The book of Acts records the expansion of the gospel from Jerusalem to the ends of the known world, as disciples like Paul, Peter, and Philip proclaimed Christ in both Jewish and gentile contexts.

This mission was not without opposition. The early church faced intense persecution from both religious authorities and the Roman government. Yet persecution often served to advance the mission, as believers scattered to new regions and shared the gospel wherever they went (Acts 8:1–4). The resilience and faithfulness of these early disciples inspired others to follow Christ, even at great personal cost.

The mission of discipleship continues to shape the church today. The example of the early church challenges contemporary believers to embrace both the internal work of spiritual growth and the external work of evangelism and service. Discipleship is not static; it is a dynamic process of being transformed by Christ and inviting others to experience his transforming power.

The early church thrived in a world that was often hostile to the gospel, yet their commitment to discipleship fueled a movement that transformed history. However, as Christianity became more culturally dominant, discipleship often became institutionalized, losing some of its depth and relational focus. Today, as we face a rapidly changing cultural landscape, the church must recover the urgency and intentionality of biblical discipleship. What does it look like to make disciples in a post-Christian world?

The Church's Mission of Discipleship Today

The mission of discipleship, given by Jesus to his apostles and embodied by the early church, remains central to the identity and purpose of the church today. The Great Commission is not an optional task but the foundation of the church's calling. Jesus's command to "make disciples of all nations" (Matt 28:19) requires a commitment to both evangelism and the ongoing spiritual formation of believers. Yet, in today's post-Christian world, this mission faces significant challenges. Secularism, relativism, individualism, and cultural distrust of religious institutions create barriers to discipleship that must be addressed with wisdom and intentionality.

Despite these challenges, the church also has extraordinary opportunities to reimagine and reinvigorate its mission. By recovering a biblical vision of discipleship, churches can build thriving, Christ-centered communities that nurture spiritual growth, form mature believers, and engage the world with the transformative power of the gospel. In this section, we will explore the key elements of discipleship today, focusing on evangelism, spiritual formation, mentorship, community, and cultural engagement.

Discipleship Begins with Evangelism

Discipleship begins with an invitation to follow Christ. Jesus's ministry regularly involved a call to repentance and belief in the good news of the kingdom (Mark 1:15). Similarly, the early church emphasized proclaiming the gospel as the first step in making disciples. Today, evangelism remains essential to the church's mission, but it requires sensitivity to the cultural realities of the twenty-first century.

In many contexts, people are increasingly disconnected from Christian traditions and skeptical of organized religion. As a result, traditional evangelistic methods—such as large public events, street preaching, or confrontational approaches—may be less effective. Instead, relational evangelism, characterized by trust-building, dialogue, and hospitality, has become increasingly important. Believers are called to bear witness to Christ through both their words and their actions, demonstrating the reality of the gospel in their relationships and daily lives.

The apostle Peter encourages Christians to be ready to explain the hope they have in Christ, "yet do it with gentleness and respect" (1 Pet 3:15). This approach to evangelism emphasizes empathy and humility, recognizing that effective witness involves listening to people's stories, understanding their doubts and concerns, and pointing them to Jesus with grace and truth. In a post-Christian world, where many people are spiritually searching but wary of dogmatism, such relational witness can open doors to discipleship.

Evangelism must also be holistic. While the proclamation of the gospel is essential, discipleship involves more than just a verbal message. Jesus's ministry combined teaching with acts of compassion, healing, and justice. Similarly, the church's mission includes addressing both spiritual and physical needs. Ministries of service, social justice, and advocacy for the vulnerable provide powerful opportunities to demonstrate God's love and invite others into a life of discipleship.

Spiritual Formation: Growing into Christlikeness

Once someone responds to the gospel, the next step in discipleship is spiritual formation. Spiritual formation is the process by which believers are transformed into the image of Christ through the power of the Holy Spirit. Paul describes this transformation in Romans 12:2, urging believers not to conform to the patterns of the world but to be "transformed by the renewal of [their] mind."

Spiritual formation involves both personal and communal practices that cultivate faith, character, and holiness. These practices include prayer, Bible study, worship, fasting, confession, and service. Through these disciplines, disciples learn to abide in Christ, allowing his life to shape their thoughts, desires, and behaviors (John 15:4–5). However, spiritual formation is not about self-improvement or earning God's favor; it is a response to God's grace, rooted in a deepening relationship with him.

The early church provides a model for integrating spiritual formation into the life of the community. Acts 2:42–47 describes how the early Christians devoted themselves to the apostles' teaching, fellowship, the breaking of bread, and prayer. These communal practices nurtured both individual and collective growth, creating an environment where discipleship could flourish. Churches today are called to cultivate similar rhythms of worship, learning, and fellowship that foster spiritual growth.

One of the greatest challenges to spiritual formation in modern culture is the busyness and distraction of daily life. Many believers struggle to prioritize time with God amid competing demands from work, family, technology, and entertainment. To counteract these pressures, churches can help disciples develop intentional practices of sabbath rest, reflection, and attentiveness to God's presence. Spiritual formation requires not only knowledge of Scripture but also a reordering of priorities around Christ.

Mentorship and Leadership Development

Mentorship and leadership development are crucial components of discipleship. Jesus modeled relational discipleship by investing deeply in a small group of disciples, and the early church continued this pattern through mentorship relationships such as Paul and Timothy. Mentorship involves walking alongside others in their spiritual journey, providing guidance, encouragement, correction, and accountability.

In today's church, mentorship can take many forms, including one-on-one relationships, small groups, and structured discipleship programs. Effective mentors are those who not only teach but also model a life of faith. Paul's exhortation to the Corinthians, "Imitate me, as I imitate Christ" (1 Cor 11:1), underscores the importance of leading by example. Mentors help disciples navigate challenges, discern their calling, and grow in spiritual maturity.

Leadership development is particularly important for sustaining the church's mission. As the early church grew, the apostles recognized the need to appoint additional leaders to oversee various ministries. In Acts 6:1–7, the apostles appoint seven men to serve as deacons, freeing the apostles to focus on teaching and prayer. This delegation of responsibility allowed the church to continue growing while ensuring that practical needs were met.

Today, churches must be intentional about identifying and training new leaders who can carry on the work of discipleship. Leadership development involves equipping individuals with theological knowledge, ministry skills, and spiritual maturity. Churches can provide opportunities for leadership training through workshops, internships, and mentorship programs. Developing leaders who are grounded in Christ and empowered by the Spirit is essential for the long-term health and mission of the church.

The Role of Christian Community

Christian community plays a vital role in discipleship, as the Christian life is not meant to be lived in isolation but within the body of Christ. From the earliest days of the church, believers have gathered together for worship, teaching, prayer, and fellowship, recognizing that spiritual growth flourishes in the context of meaningful relationships. The New Testament consistently describes the church as a family, a body, and a temple, emphasizing the deep interconnectedness of its members. In Romans 12:4–5, Paul reminds believers that they are "one body in Christ, and individually members one of another," illustrating that discipleship is not simply a private endeavor but a shared pursuit of faithfulness. Similarly, Ephesians 2:19–22 presents the church as the household of God, built upon Christ as the cornerstone, where each believer is a living stone contributing to the whole. These images convey the biblical truth that Christian growth is meant to take place within the rich soil of community, where mutual encouragement, accountability, and love shape disciples into the image of Christ.

Community provides both support and accountability for spiritual growth. In a world where faith can often feel like an individual journey, the church stands as a living reminder that believers are not alone. When disciples walk together, they strengthen one another through prayer, shared wisdom, and the bearing of burdens. Hebrews 10:24–25 exhorts believers to "consider how to stir up one another to love and good works, not neglecting to meet together, as is the habit of some, but encouraging one another." This encouragement is essential, particularly in a culture where many struggle with doubt, discouragement, and the pressures of secularism. In a healthy Christian community, believers can share their struggles without fear of condemnation, celebrate spiritual victories together, and receive encouragement to persevere through trials. Furthermore, the communal nature of discipleship allows for the diversity of spiritual gifts to be exercised for the common good. Paul, in 1 Corinthians 12:4–7, teaches that God has given different gifts to different members of the church, ensuring that the body of Christ is built up through teaching, serving, exhorting, and acts of mercy. Discipleship, then, is not solely the work of pastors or teachers but a calling for every believer to contribute to the growth of others.

However, building authentic Christian community requires intentionality. In a fragmented and individualistic society, many people feel isolated, disconnected, and unsure of where they truly belong. Churches must actively create spaces where deep relationships can form and flourish, recognizing that real community does not happen automatically. Small groups provide an intimate setting for shared discipleship, where believers can study Scripture, pray together, and support one another in their spiritual journeys. Fellowship events, service opportunities, and mission projects foster bonds between members, as working together for a common purpose builds unity and strengthens relationships.

One of the most powerful tools in fostering community is the practice of hospitality. Hospitality is more than hosting events; it is a mindset of openness and welcome, where both believers and seekers are invited into a place of grace, belonging, and shared life. Jesus modeled this in his ministry, sharing meals with sinners and outcasts, demonstrating that the kingdom of God is a place of radical welcome and transformation. In the same way, the church must embody a spirit of hospitality, inviting people into authentic relationships where they can experience the love of Christ through his people.

Discipleship in the New Testament was never merely an individual pursuit of faith but was intrinsically linked to the gathered body of believers. From the earliest days of the church, the practice of discipleship was centered around the communal worship of God. Acts 2:42–47 describes how the first Christians devoted themselves to the apostles' teaching, fellowship, the breaking of bread, and prayer—activities that were not only formative but also acts of worship. The early disciples did not simply learn doctrine in isolation; they gathered regularly to worship, hear the word preached, partake in the sacraments, and pray together. These gatherings were not secondary to their discipleship but were the very means through which they were shaped into Christ's likeness. Worship was where they encountered God's presence, where their hearts were reoriented toward his kingdom, and where they were reminded of their identity as his people. The pattern of discipleship in the New Testament is inseparable from corporate worship because worship is where the church collectively submits to the authority of Christ, receives his grace, and responds with devotion and obedience.

In corporate worship, discipleship reaches its highest expression as believers not only grow in knowledge and holiness but also offer their entire lives as a sacrifice of praise to God (Rom 12:1). Worship is the context in which faith is strengthened, imaginations are shaped by divine realities, and the bonds of Christian community are deepened. The weekly gathering of the church is not just an obligation but the lifeblood of discipleship, reorienting believers to God's truth, forming them in love, and sending them out to bear witness in the world. As the church engages in worship, it is not only fulfilling its calling in the present but anticipating the ultimate reality of the heavenly kingdom, where discipleship will give way to the unceasing worship of the triune God.

The Biblical Vision of Discipleship

As we have seen in this first chapter, the biblical vision of discipleship is comprehensive, shaping the whole person—mind, heart, and body—in conformity to Christ. Or, in the words of C. S. Lewis, "the Church exists for nothing else but to draw men into Christ, to make them little Christs."[1] It begins with God's call to Abraham to trust and follow him, continues through the covenantal relationship established with Israel at Mount Sinai, and finds its ultimate fulfillment in the life, ministry, and teaching of Jesus Christ. Discipleship is not merely about personal faith or moral improvement; it is about being caught up in the grand narrative of redemption, transformed by the Spirit, and commissioned to participate in Christ's mission of making disciples of all nations.

While the church's mission of discipleship remains unchanged, the world around us has shifted dramatically. The assumptions that once supported faith are fading, and skepticism, relativism, and secularism present new obstacles to forming mature disciples. How should we respond? If discipleship is to thrive in the modern world, we must understand the cultural forces shaping people's hearts and minds. In the chapters that follow, we will explore how discipleship in a post-Christian age requires engaging both the mind and heart. Drawing on the insights of Lewis's cultural apologetics, we will examine how reason, imagination, and community can serve as essential pillars for forming resilient disciples today.

---

1. Lewis, *Mere Christianity*, 171.

Chapter 3

The Cultural Context of C. S. Lewis

To understand how C. S. Lewis's cultural apologetics can aid the church's mission of discipleship today, it is vital to grasp the world in which he lived and the challenges he faced. Lewis's context—marked by the trauma of war, the rise of secularism, and the dominance of relativism—shaped his apologetic approach and his deep concern for addressing both the rational and imaginative dimensions of faith. His personal journey from atheism to Christianity gave him a unique ability to engage skeptics empathetically, offering answers to questions he had once wrestled with himself.

This chapter explores three key dimensions of Lewis's cultural context: first, the impact of war, secularism, and relativism; second, Lewis's personal spiritual journey from unbelief to faith; and third, the intellectual challenges he sought to address through his writings. Understanding these influences helps illuminate the power and relevance of Lewis's apologetics for discipleship today.

Lewis's World: War, Secularism, and Relativism

Lewis lived through one of the most turbulent periods in modern history, a time marked by the devastation of two world wars, the rise of secularism, and the spread of moral relativism.[1] These cultural forces profoundly

---

1. Lewis addressed the dangers of secularism and moral relativism in *The Abolition of Man* (1943), where he critiques the rejection of objective moral values, and in *Mere*

shaped the intellectual and spiritual climate of the early to mid-twentieth century, influencing both the challenges Lewis faced and the apologetic strategies he developed to address them. In this context, traditional Christian beliefs were increasingly questioned and dismissed by many intellectuals and ordinary people alike. War exposed the fragility of human civilization, secularism undermined faith in a transcendent moral order, and relativism challenged the very concept of objective truth. Lewis's response to these forces demonstrates his deep understanding of the cultural moment and his ability to engage both the mind and the heart in defense of Christian discipleship.

The Trauma of War: The Shattering of Optimism

Few events in human history have been as destructive and disillusioning as the two world wars of the twentieth century. The First World War (1914–1918) shattered the optimism that had characterized much of the nineteenth century, a period often referred to as the "Age of Progress." Before the war, Western intellectuals largely believed that human reason, scientific discovery, and technological advancement would lead to an era of peace and prosperity. This faith in human progress was deeply rooted in the Enlightenment ideals that had shaped modern society. Many assumed that education, rational governance, and economic development would gradually eliminate war, poverty, and suffering, ushering in a golden age of civilization.

However, World War I proved to be a devastating rebuke to such optimism. The war introduced a new level of mechanized violence and destruction that was unlike anything the world had seen before. Soldiers endured the nightmare of trench warfare, suffering through relentless artillery bombardments, machine-gun fire, and the horrors of chemical weapons such as mustard gas. Millions of young men—many of whom had entered the war with patriotic enthusiasm and a sense of duty—were killed or left

---

Christianity (1952), which was originally a series of BBC wartime radio talks responding to the moral and spiritual crises of his time. His satirical work *The Screwtape Letters* (1942) further exposes how modern distractions and ideological trends undermine faith, while *Present Concerns: Journalistic Essays* (1986) offers insights into his reflections on war, education, and the impact of secular thought. For historical and cultural context, Alister McGrath's *C. S. Lewis – A Life: Eccentric Genius, Reluctant Prophet* (2013) provides an in-depth biography, while George Marsden's *C. S. Lewis's "Mere Christianity": A Biography* (2016) explores how Lewis's engagement with secularism shaped his most famous apologetic work.

permanently scarred, both physically and mentally. The mechanization of warfare dehumanized combat, reducing soldiers to mere numbers in a vast and impersonal struggle between empires. The staggering death toll, coupled with the psychological devastation of those who survived, left societies grappling with grief, trauma, and a profound sense of disillusionment.

Lewis was among those whose lives were directly shaped by the war. In 1917, at the age of 19, he enlisted in the British Army and was commissioned as a second lieutenant. Like many young men of his generation, he found himself thrust into the brutal realities of trench warfare on the Western Front in France. In 1918, during the Battle of Arras, Lewis was wounded by shrapnel and sent back to England to recover. Although he rarely spoke publicly about his wartime experiences, the trauma left an indelible mark on his worldview. His later writings, particularly *The Screwtape Letters* and *The Problem of Pain*, reflect his deep wrestling with the moral and existential questions raised by human suffering and evil.

Beyond its personal impact, the war had sweeping cultural and philosophical consequences. Across Europe and the United States, many lost faith in the moral and spiritual foundations of Western civilization. The war exposed the dark side of human nature, revealing the capacity for unparalleled cruelty, greed, and destruction. Intellectuals and artists responded by expressing their disillusionment in literature, philosophy, and art, rejecting the idealism of the past. The so-called "Lost Generation" of writers—including Ernest Hemingway, F. Scott Fitzgerald, and T. S. Eliot—captured themes of alienation, despair, and the collapse of meaning. Eliot's *The Waste Land* (1922) reflected the spiritual and cultural fragmentation of the postwar world, depicting a civilization stripped of hope, faith, and coherence.

This growing skepticism led many to turn away from traditional religion, believing that the existence of a good and omnipotent God was incompatible with the sheer scale of suffering they had witnessed. The First World War became a catalyst for the rise of atheism, existentialism, and agnosticism. The idea that moral progress was inevitable now seemed naïve, and scientific naturalism and materialism gained increasing influence as alternative explanations for human nature and history. Many intellectuals and philosophers, including Bertrand Russell and Sigmund Freud, openly questioned the validity of religious belief, suggesting that faith was a mere illusion or a psychological crutch.[2]

---

2. Russell, in *Why I Am Not a Christian* (1957) and *Religion and Science* (1935), argues that religious belief is rooted in irrational fears rather than reason and that science

However, the Second World War (1939–1945) deepened these existential crises even further. If World War I had been devastating, World War II revealed the full depths of human depravity. The Holocaust—the systematic extermination of six million Jews and millions of others by the Nazi regime—shocked the world with its calculated, industrialized brutality. The war also saw the indiscriminate bombing of civilian populations, the use of nuclear weapons on Hiroshima and Nagasaki, and the displacement of millions of refugees. The scale of destruction forced society to confront not just the reality of human suffering, but the terrifying capacity for evil within humanity itself.

Unlike many intellectuals who responded to the war with further despair and cynicism, Lewis took a different path. Rather than retreating into pessimism, he sought to offer a compelling vision of hope and meaning through the Christian faith. During World War II, Lewis became a public voice for Christianity, delivering a series of BBC radio talks that were later compiled into *Mere Christianity*. In these talks, Lewis did not ignore or downplay the problem of evil and suffering; rather, he confronted it head-on, arguing that Christianity provides not only an explanation for human sin but also a message of redemption. He suggested that the very fact that we recognize evil as "wrong" points to a moral standard beyond ourselves, a reality that secular worldviews could not adequately explain.

For many listeners, Lewis's calm and reasoned approach provided a source of comfort and inspiration in a time of crisis. Unlike existentialist thinkers who saw suffering as meaningless, Lewis affirmed that suffering, while painful, was not purposeless. He spoke of God's ultimate sovereignty, of how trials and hardships could refine human character, and of how suffering pointed to humanity's need for divine grace and restoration. His wartime talks reached thousands of listeners, some of whom had lost family members in the Blitz, others who were facing the constant threat of death on the battlefield. His words offered not escapism, but a firm foundation of faith in a world that seemed to be falling apart.

Through his own experiences of war, Lewis understood that Christianity had to address the real struggles of human existence. He rejected both shallow optimism and absolute despair, instead offering a faith that could

---

provides a more reliable means of understanding reality. Similarly, Freud, in *The Future of an Illusion* (1927), claims that religion is a psychological construct born from humanity's need for security and paternal protection. These perspectives have influenced later secular thinkers such as Richard Dawkins and Christopher Hitchens, who argue that religious faith is an outdated and harmful delusion.

withstand suffering without being broken by it. His ability to articulate a rational yet deeply personal defense of faith made him one of the most influential Christian thinkers of the twentieth century.

The trauma of the two world wars permanently reshaped Western culture, philosophy, and religious thought. Many intellectuals and ordinary people alike struggled to reconcile the reality of suffering with the existence of God. Yet, while many abandoned faith, Lewis found in Christianity not only a coherent answer to suffering but also a profound hope that transcended it. His wartime writings reflect his conviction that, even in the darkest times, the light of Christ still shines, offering redemption to a world in desperate need of it.

The Rise of Secularism and the Decline of Religious Authority

Another major force shaping Lewis's world was the rise of secularism. The early twentieth century witnessed a profound transformation in the intellectual and cultural landscape of the Western world, one that increasingly marginalized religious belief and authority. The rise of secularism was not merely a rejection of specific religious doctrines but a broader shift in worldview, where faith was increasingly seen as irrational, outdated, and unnecessary. This movement was driven by scientific advancements, philosophical developments, and social changes, all of which contributed to the growing perception that religion belonged to the past rather than the future.

One of the most significant forces behind the rise of secularism was the success of the scientific revolution, which had dramatically expanded humanity's understanding of the natural world. Figures such as Isaac Newton, Charles Darwin, and Albert Einstein revolutionized the way people understood the workings of the universe. The discoveries of Newtonian mechanics in the seventeenth century suggested that the cosmos operated according to fixed, rational laws, seemingly reducing the need for divine intervention in explaining natural phenomena. However, it was Darwin's theory of evolution by natural selection, published in *On the Origin of Species* (1859), that most directly challenged traditional religious explanations of human origins. Many intellectuals interpreted Darwin's work as eliminating the need for a Creator, reinforcing the idea that life and humanity itself were products of blind, impersonal forces rather than divine design.

As scientific knowledge advanced, some thinkers concluded that religious explanations were not only unnecessary but unscientific, relegating faith to the realm of superstition. This perspective became particularly dominant in elite academic and cultural institutions, where naturalism—the belief that everything can be explained in terms of natural causes without reference to the supernatural—became the prevailing intellectual framework.

The Enlightenment of the eighteenth century had already laid the philosophical groundwork for secularism by emphasizing reason, autonomy, and skepticism toward traditional authority. Philosophers such as Voltaire, Immanuel Kant, and David Hume suggested that human beings could discover truth and moral principles through rational inquiry, rather than relying on divine revelation. Kant's emphasis on individual autonomy reinforced the growing sentiment that morality and meaning should be derived from reason alone. Meanwhile, Hume's empirical skepticism cast doubt on miracles and divine intervention, further eroding confidence in religious claims.[3]

By the time Lewis entered adulthood, secularism had become deeply entrenched in Western thought, particularly in universities and intellectual circles. The rise of materialism—the belief that only physical matter exists and that all phenomena can be explained through natural causes—became a dominant worldview.

Lewis, as a young man, was deeply influenced by these secular and materialist ideas. He adopted an atheistic worldview, convinced that the universe was cold, indifferent, and governed by impersonal forces. In *Surprised by Joy*, he later described this period of his life as spiritually bleak and devoid of meaning. He saw the cosmos as a vast, impersonal machine, and human life as a brief accident in an indifferent universe. To Lewis, at the time, religion seemed to be little more than wishful thinking, a desperate attempt to impose meaning on an otherwise meaningless existence.

---

3. Voltaire, Immanuel Kant, and David Hume were key figures in the Enlightenment who challenged the necessity of divine revelation for knowledge and morality. Voltaire, in works such as *Philosophical Dictionary*, critiqued religious dogma and argued for reason as the foundation of human progress. Kant, in *Religion Within the Bounds of Mere Reason*, maintained that moral principles could be derived from human reason alone, independent of theological authority. Hume, in *Dialogues Concerning Natural Religion*, cast doubt on traditional arguments for God's existence and emphasized empirical skepticism as a means of discerning truth. Together, these thinkers contributed to a shift in Western thought, where reason was increasingly seen as self-sufficient in matters of ethics and knowledge, apart from religious belief.

The Spread of Moral Relativism

This secular worldview had far-reaching consequences beyond intellectual belief. The decline of religious authority also reshaped the moral landscape of Western society. For centuries, Christian teachings had provided the foundation for moral norms, shaping concepts of justice, human dignity, and ethical responsibility. However, as belief in a transcendent moral order declined, many began to question the foundations of ethical norms themselves. If there was no divine lawgiver, what basis remained for distinguishing between right and wrong? Nietzsche famously declared that "God is dead," warning that the collapse of religious belief would lead to moral relativism and nihilism. Without an external source of moral authority, he argued, humanity would be forced to invent its own values or abandon the pursuit of meaning altogether.[4]

As faith in a transcendent moral order declined, so too did the idea that moral principles were objective, absolute, and binding on all people. Instead, relativism proposed that moral values are fluid, socially constructed, and culturally contingent. According to this perspective, what is considered "right" or "wrong" is not determined by any universal standard but varies across societies and historical periods. No single moral framework, relativists argued, could claim absolute authority over human behavior.

This shift represented a fundamental break from the traditional understanding of morality that had long been anchored in Judeo-Christian principles. Historically, moral law was seen as grounded in God's character, providing a fixed and universal standard by which all human actions were judged. However, as scientific naturalism, secularism, and materialism gained influence, many intellectuals began to argue that morality was not divinely revealed but rather a human construct shaped by social, psychological, and evolutionary forces.

By the early twentieth century, relativism had become increasingly influential in academic and cultural discourse. Anthropologists such as Franz Boas and Ruth Benedict challenged the idea that any one moral system could be considered superior to another, emphasizing the diversity of

---

4. Nietzsche warned that the absence of a divine moral standard would force humanity to either construct new values or face nihilism—the belief that life lacks inherent meaning or purpose. His ideas profoundly influenced existentialist and postmodern thought, laying the groundwork for the rejection of universal moral principles in favor of subjective ethical frameworks. See Nietzsche, *The Gay Science* (1974); *Thus Spoke Zarathustra* (1978).

ethical traditions across different societies. They argued that moral judgments should be understood within the context of specific cultures, rather than imposed as universal truths. This perspective undermined the idea of absolute moral laws, reinforcing the notion that ethics were fluid, adaptable, and subject to cultural evolution.[5]

At the same time, existentialist philosophers such as Jean-Paul Sartre and Albert Camus explored the implications of a world without objective moral truths. Sartre argued that human beings were "condemned to be free," meaning that in a universe without divine authority, individuals were solely responsible for creating their own meaning, values, and purpose. Camus, in works such as *The Stranger* and *The Myth of Sisyphus*, portrayed human existence as a struggle against the absurdity of a meaningless universe, where moral choices were ultimately arbitrary. These ideas permeated literature, art, and popular culture, reinforcing a worldview in which morality was seen as subjective rather than fixed.[6]

Lewis viewed the rise of moral relativism with deep concern. He believed that the rejection of objective moral values would lead to the dehumanization of society, where ethical principles would become dictated by power, convenience, or individual preference rather than rooted in an external reality. In *The Abolition of Man*, published in 1944 in the middle of World War II, Lewis warned that without a shared moral foundation, individuals would be driven by their own desires and easily manipulated by those in power. He argued that relativism ultimately undermined human dignity, making morality a matter of personal or societal whim rather than an immutable standard.

For Lewis, moral truth was not an arbitrary social construct, but something woven into the fabric of reality. He referred to this universal moral law as "the Tao," representing the idea that certain moral principles—such as justice, honesty, and mercy—are intrinsically known to all human beings, regardless of culture or time period. He demonstrated how moral absolutes could be found across different civilizations, suggesting that objective morality was a reflection of divine truth rather than a mere product of social conditioning.

---

5. See Franz Boas, *The Mind of Primitive Man* (1911); Ruth Benedict, *Patterns of Culture* (1934); Richard J. Perry, *Anthropology and the Racial Politics of Culture* (2011).

6. See Sartre, *Existentialism Is a Humanism* (2007); Camus, *The Myth of Sisyphus* (1991).

Therefore, the world in which Lewis lived was shaped by the trauma of war, the rise of secularism, and the spread of relativism. These forces created a context in which traditional Christian beliefs were increasingly questioned, marginalized, or outright rejected. However, Lewis did not respond to these challenges by retreating into nostalgia or dogmatic rigidity. Instead, he engaged the intellectual and cultural climate of his time with rigorous reasoning, deep imagination, and a genuine concern for the modern soul.

His work remains relevant because the challenges he confronted are still with us today. Secularism continues to erode religious belief, relativism continues to challenge moral objectivity, and the search for meaning remains as urgent as ever. Lewis's defense of objective moral law and the necessity of Christian discipleship continues to offer a powerful alternative to the fragmented, relativistic worldview that dominates much of contemporary culture. His writings remind us that Christianity is not just a set of private beliefs but a vision of reality that speaks to the fundamental nature of truth, morality, and the purpose of human life.

Lewis's Personal Journey from Atheism to Faith

Lewis's journey from atheism to Christianity is a compelling story of intellectual struggle, spiritual longing, and transformative encounters with truth. This journey was not a sudden or purely emotional experience; rather, it was a gradual process shaped by a series of pivotal moments and relationships. Lewis's conversion was driven by both rational inquiry and the persistent pull of an indescribable longing for something greater—a longing he later identified as a desire for God. His journey provides a powerful model for engaging skeptics in discipleship, demonstrating the integration of reason, imagination, and personal experience in the process of coming to faith.[7]

---

[7]. C. S. Lewis recounts his journey from atheism to faith in *Surprised by Joy* (1955), his spiritual autobiography that details his intellectual and emotional struggles leading to his conversion to Christianity. *Mere Christianity* (1952), though primarily an apologetic work, also contains insights into his conversion process and the rational arguments that persuaded him of Christianity's truth. His letters, collected in *Collected Letters of C. S. Lewis: Volume 1, Family Letters 1905–1931* and *Collected Letters of C. S. Lewis: Volume 2, Books, Broadcasts, and the War 1931–1949*, provide firsthand reflections on his transition from atheism to theism and ultimately to Christianity. Alister McGrath's *C. S. Lewis – A Life: Eccentric Genius, Reluctant Prophet* offers a comprehensive biography that carefully

Early Life: The Seeds of Doubt

Lewis was born on November 29, 1898, in Belfast, Ireland, into a culturally Protestant household that placed a strong emphasis on education, literature, and intellectual exploration. His parents, Albert and Florence Lewis, were both well-read and highly educated, creating an environment where books were not merely objects of study but gateways to adventure and discovery. From an early age, Lewis displayed a remarkable imagination and an insatiable curiosity about the world. He and his older brother, Warren ("Warnie"), spent countless hours crafting intricate fantasy worlds, weaving together stories filled with mythical creatures, noble quests, and heroic battles. This early love for myth and fantasy would remain a defining characteristic of his intellectual and spiritual journey, later playing a crucial role in how he came to understand Christianity as the "true myth."

Despite the intellectual richness of his early years, Lewis's childhood was marked by profound loss and emotional upheaval. In 1908, when he was just nine years old, his mother died of cancer, a tragedy that shook the very foundation of his young world. The pain of this loss was compounded by his fervent prayers for her healing, which went unanswered, leaving him with an overwhelming sense of abandonment and confusion. The God he had been taught to believe in—a loving and sovereign Father—suddenly seemed distant, indifferent, and unresponsive to human suffering. In later years, Lewis would reflect on this event as the first major blow to his childhood faith, planting in him the seeds of skepticism, doubt, and a deep intellectual wrestling with the problem of pain.

Adding to his grief was the reaction of his father, Albert, who, devastated by his wife's death, withdrew into his own sorrow. Emotionally distant and struggling with his own loss, Albert became increasingly detached from his sons, leaving Lewis feeling profoundly alone. This emotional isolation had a lasting impact on him, reinforcing a growing sense that the universe was cold and indifferent to human suffering. In many ways, his personal experience mirrored the philosophical problem he

---

examines Lewis's intellectual and emotional path to faith, including his dialogues with Christian friends such as J. R. R. Tolkien. George Sayer's *Jack: A Life of C. S. Lewis* (1994) provides a close, personal account of Lewis's conversion, written by someone who knew him well. Alan Jacobs's *The Narnian: The Life and Imagination of C. S. Lewis* (2008) places Lewis's conversion in the broader context of his imaginative life and intellectual influences. David C. Downing's *The Most Reluctant Convert: C. S. Lewis's Journey to Faith* (2002) delves deeply into the philosophical and emotional struggles that shaped his spiritual transformation.

would later articulate in *The Problem of Pain*: if God is both good and powerful, why does He allow suffering?

In the wake of his mother's death, Lewis was sent to Wynyard School in Watford, the first of several English boarding schools he would attend. These institutions, rather than offering solace or intellectual enrichment, only deepened his alienation. Wynyard was a bleak and oppressive place, run by a headmaster whose cruelty and erratic behavior made the environment almost unbearable. The harsh discipline and rigid structure of school life left Lewis disillusioned, particularly with the version of Christianity he encountered there. Faith, instead of being a source of wonder and joy, was presented to him as a system of rigid moralism and empty rituals. He later wrote that he saw little connection between the lifeless religious practices imposed upon him and the vibrant world of imagination he cherished in literature and mythology.

As he progressed in his education, Lewis's skepticism toward religion deepened. At Cherbourg School and later Malvern College, he encountered scientific naturalism and materialist philosophy, which seemed to offer a more rational and empirical explanation of reality than religious belief. Darwinian evolution, the growing prestige of modern science, and the influence of rationalist thinkers led him to embrace atheism with increasing confidence. He saw religious belief as a relic of the past, a comforting illusion that had been necessary in a more ignorant age but was now discredited by reason, logic, and empirical evidence.

The Intellectual Foundations of Lewis's Atheism

Lewis's atheism was not merely a reaction against personal disappointments with religion; it was deeply rooted in the dominant intellectual movements of his time. He was profoundly influenced by scientific materialism, naturalism, and the rationalist philosophy that had gained prominence in the late nineteenth and early twentieth centuries. The remarkable success of modern science in explaining natural phenomena had led many intellectuals to conclude that the supernatural was unnecessary—that the world operated as a closed system governed solely by physical laws.

Lewis absorbed these ideas deeply and, by the time he entered Oxford University in 1917, he had embraced a firmly materialist and mechanistic view of the world. To him, the cosmos was a vast, impersonal machine, operating according to fixed natural laws without room for divine intervention or supernatural purpose. Human consciousness, he believed, was nothing more than a byproduct of physical processes, and concepts such as meaning, morality, and beauty were ultimately subjective and illusory. His reading of rationalist thinkers such as H. G. Wells and Bertrand Russell reinforced his belief that religion was a relic of a less enlightened age, an attempt to explain mysteries that science had since illuminated.

At the heart of Lewis's atheism was the problem of evil and suffering, a philosophical challenge that deeply troubled him. If a benevolent and omnipotent God existed, why did so much pain, injustice, and cruelty pervade the world? The horrors of World War I, which Lewis personally witnessed as a soldier, seemed to confirm his worst suspicions: that the universe was indifferent to human suffering and that belief in a good and just God was untenable in the face of overwhelming evil.

Yet, even as Lewis found intellectual satisfaction in atheism, he could not escape moments of deep, inexplicable longing—what he later called "Joy." These experiences often came unexpectedly, sparked by encounters with beauty, literature, nature, or music. The sight of a breathtaking landscape, a passage in Norse mythology, or a moving piece of poetry would awaken in him a fleeting but powerful sense of something beyond the material world—a reality that was more real, more beautiful, and more significant than anything he had encountered in his rationalist framework.

This paradox haunted Lewis. On the one hand, he was convinced that the universe was cold and mechanical, devoid of purpose or supernatural reality. On the other hand, his deepest, most profound experiences pointed to something beyond material existence, something that seemed truer than the atheistic worldview he had embraced. He found himself torn between his intellectual allegiance to materialism and his personal encounters with something that defied it.

This conflict would remain unresolved for many years. Lewis tried to rationalize his experiences of Joy, dismissing them as psychological artifacts or mere nostalgic illusions. Yet, no matter how much he sought to suppress or explain them away, these moments of transcendent longing continued to return, undermining his certainty that materialism could provide a complete and satisfactory account of reality.

Ultimately, this paradox—the tension between his intellectual atheism and his imaginative yearning for something beyond it—would become one of the key forces driving his eventual conversion. Rather than being a weakness in his atheistic worldview, Lewis began to see that his longing for meaning and transcendence might, in fact, be pointing to something real. His journey toward faith would not be a sudden rejection of reason but a reexamination of reality in light of both reason and experience. What began as a confident embrace of atheism would eventually become one of the most reluctant yet profound conversions to Christianity of the twentieth century.

The Influence of Literature and Myth

Throughout Lewis's early life and education, literature played a pivotal role in shaping his imagination, intellectual development, and eventual journey toward faith. From childhood, he was enthralled by stories, particularly mythology, fantasy, and epic poetry, which seemed to awaken something deep within him. Even as he moved toward atheism in his adolescence, his love for myth and storytelling never faded. Instead, it created a tension within him—one that would later become central to his conversion.

Lewis was particularly drawn to the great myths of the past, including *The Iliad* and *The Odyssey, Beowulf,* Norse mythology, and the Arthurian legends. These stories, filled with heroism, sacrifice, destiny, and the battle between good and evil, stirred within him a longing for something beyond the material world. He would later identify this longing as *Sehnsucht,* a German word meaning a deep yearning for something unknown yet profoundly significant. Even as he denied the supernatural, he found himself emotionally and imaginatively moved by these mythic narratives—stories that pointed to themes of redemption, sacrifice, and transcendent meaning.

One of the most transformative literary encounters in Lewis's life came when he read *Phantastes,* a fantasy novel by George MacDonald. MacDonald's writing was imbued with a sense of the numinous, a world where spiritual realities and moral truths were woven seamlessly into the fabric of the narrative. Lewis later described this experience as a baptism of his imagination, awakening in him a new way of seeing reality. Even though he remained an atheist at the time, MacDonald's work subtly undermined his materialist assumptions, suggesting that perhaps reality itself contained deeper layers of meaning than he had previously allowed.

Yet, despite his love for these mythic stories, Lewis continued to view Christianity as just another myth—one among many. In his atheistic framework, myths were beautiful, but they were not true. He saw them as cultural artifacts, expressions of human creativity that conveyed symbolic meaning but had no basis in actual reality. At the same time, however, he could not ignore the profound power of myth. He recognized that these stories had a universal quality, expressing truths about human nature, morality, and destiny that transcended time and culture. He admired how myths captured the deepest longings of the human soul, but he struggled to reconcile this appreciation with his commitment to a rationalist, materialist view of the world.

This internal conflict between reason and imagination became even more pronounced during his studies at University College, Oxford. Lewis excelled academically, displaying a brilliant mind for philosophy, history, and literature. He would go on to become a fellow and tutor in English literature at Magdalen College, where his knowledge of classical and medieval literature deepened. Yet, despite his intellectual success, he remained spiritually restless.

The experiences of "joy"—those fleeting moments of intense longing and beauty—continued to haunt him. No matter how much he tried to explain them away as psychological phenomena, they persisted. These moments were often triggered by literary passages, poetry, or mythic stories, suggesting to him that his materialist framework was insufficient to explain the full range of human experience. His love for myth clashed with his rejection of the supernatural, leaving him with a growing sense that perhaps the world was more than just atoms and empty space.

Lewis's increasing discomfort with the limitations of materialism would eventually lead him to reexamine his assumptions about truth and meaning. His journey toward faith did not begin with a sudden religious experience or an emotional conversion, but rather a deep intellectual struggle to reconcile his love for myth with his atheistic worldview. In the end, it was literature itself—the very thing that had shaped his mind and imagination from childhood—that would ultimately open the door to belief in something greater than himself.

Friendships and the Challenge of Christian Thought

A turning point in Lewis's spiritual journey came not through an isolated moment of revelation but through his friendships with several Christian intellectuals who challenged his worldview. Chief among these were J. R. R. Tolkien and Hugo Dyson, both of whom were members of the Inklings, a literary discussion group at Oxford University. These friendships provided Lewis with something he had not yet encountered in his intellectual circles—a rigorous, thoughtful, and deeply rational defense of Christianity from people he deeply respected.

Tolkien, a devout Catholic, played an especially significant role in Lewis's shift from atheism to theism, and eventually to Christianity. Lewis had long believed that Christianity was simply another myth, a beautiful but fictional story that contained moral truths but was not rooted in historical reality. Tolkien, however, challenged this assumption in one of the most pivotal conversations of Lewis's life.

During a famous late-night walk in September 1931, Lewis, Tolkien, and Hugo Dyson engaged in a profound discussion about myth, truth, and the nature of Christianity. Tolkien argued that myths were not lies, as Lewis had assumed, but rather human attempts to express deep spiritual truths about reality. He explained that all great myths contained echoes of divine truth, pointing to universal themes of sacrifice, redemption, and the struggle between good and evil. The difference with Christianity, he claimed, was that it was the myth that actually happened—a true myth, where God entered history in the person of Jesus Christ.

This idea was life-changing for Lewis. For years, he had been deeply moved by mythology and literature, recognizing that these stories awakened something within him—an intense longing, a desire for transcendence. Now, Tolkien was presenting him with a staggering possibility: that this longing was not arbitrary or meaningless, but a signpost to something real. Christianity, rather than being merely another inspiring tale, was the fulfillment of the deepest longings of the human heart, validated not only through its resonance with mythic archetypes but also through historical fact.

Lewis was also deeply influenced by other Christian thinkers whose writings provided him with intellectual and historical arguments for Christianity. One of the most impactful was G. K. Chesterton, whose book *The Everlasting Man* presented a compelling case for the uniqueness of Christ and the essential role of Christianity in shaping human civilization. Chesterton's argument that the incarnation was the turning point of history resonated with Lewis, who found his reasoning difficult to refute.

Through these friendships and encounters with Christian thought, Lewis gradually began to reconsider his atheism. He realized that materialism—the belief that only physical matter exists—could not provide a sufficient foundation for reason, morality, or beauty. He saw that his own rational faculties, his ability to distinguish between good and evil, and his deep longing for something beyond the material world all pointed to the existence of a divine Creator.

This shift in thinking was not instantaneous but marked the beginning of the end for Lewis's atheism. The rational objections he had held for years were being dismantled piece by piece, not through blind faith, but through rigorous intellectual engagement. He began to see that Christianity was not an anti-intellectual superstition but a worldview that could withstand scrutiny, integrating both the rational and imaginative dimensions of human experience.

The impact of these friendships was immeasurable. Tolkien, Dyson, and others had provided a space for Lewis to wrestle with his doubts without fear of dismissal. They had demonstrated that faith was not opposed to reason but was, in fact, its fulfillment. It was through these friendships that Lewis came to see Christianity not as a myth to be discarded, but as the true myth that made sense of everything else.

Conversion to Theism and Christianity

Lewis's conversion was not an instant revelation but a gradual process of intellectual and spiritual surrender, occurring in two distinct stages. His journey toward faith was marked by deep internal conflict, rigorous intellectual struggle, and moments of profound personal realization. The first stage of his conversion was his acceptance of theism—the belief in a divine being. The second, more transformative stage, was his acceptance of Jesus Christ as Lord and Savior.

By 1929, after years of resisting the implications of his changing worldview, Lewis reluctantly conceded that God existed. This was not a joyous or emotional moment but an admission that his philosophical arguments for atheism had collapsed under scrutiny. In *Surprised by Joy*, he famously described himself as "the most dejected and reluctant convert in all England."[8] His surrender to theism was not based on a sudden religious experience or an emotional crisis; rather, it was the unavoidable conclusion of his reasoning. He realized that he could no longer deny the reality of a transcendent moral and rational order, which pointed unmistakably to the existence of God.

---

8. Lewis, *Surprised by Joy*, 266.

However, at this stage, Lewis was not yet a Christian. He viewed God as an abstract, distant presence, a necessary foundation for morality and rational thought but not yet the personal God revealed in Jesus Christ. He was drawn to theism on intellectual grounds, but the idea of Christ as the Son of God and the fulfillment of human longing still seemed distant to him.

The decisive turning point came in September 1931 during a conversation with Tolkien and Dyson. The discussion revolved around the historical credibility of the New Testament and the person of Jesus Christ. Tolkien and Dyson challenged Lewis to consider why he was so deeply moved by mythic stories of sacrifice and redemption yet refused to see their ultimate fulfillment in Christianity, the one myth that was also historical fact. They argued that the story of Christ's life, death, and resurrection was not simply another religious legend but the central event in human history—one that actually happened in time and space.

This conversation profoundly unsettled Lewis. He had always valued myth and story for their deep truths, but now he was faced with the realization that the Christian narrative was not merely symbolic but objectively true. In the days following this conversation, Lewis wrestled with the implications of Christ's identity, struggling to reconcile his reason, his imagination, and his deep-seated longing for meaning.

Shortly afterward, he experienced a quiet but definitive realization while riding to Whipsnade Zoo with his brother Warren. Reflecting on the journey years later, he described how he set out that morning without belief in Christ but, by the time he arrived at the zoo, he had become a Christian. This was not an emotional epiphany but a moment of clarity and surrender, where he finally accepted the reality of Jesus Christ as Lord.

Lewis's conversion brought not only peace and fulfillment but also a renewed sense of purpose. He dedicated himself to studying theology, defending the faith, and articulating Christianity in ways that resonated with both skeptics and believers. His writings—including *Mere Christianity*, *The Problem of Pain*, and *The Chronicles of Narnia*—reflected his conviction that Christianity was not only true but also deeply transformative.

His journey from atheism to faith exemplifies the integration of reason, imagination, and personal experience in the process of discipleship. His own struggles with doubt, suffering, and the search for meaning gave him a unique ability to empathize with skeptics, making his apologetics both intellectually rigorous and personally compelling.

The Relevance of Lewis's Responses Today

The cultural challenges that Lewis addressed in his time remain highly relevant in the twenty-first century. Though the world has changed in many ways since Lewis wrote, the core issues of secularism, skepticism toward religion, relativism, and the problem of suffering persist with undiminished force. The dominant worldview in much of the Western world remains shaped by materialism, scientific naturalism, and postmodern relativism, leading many to question the foundations of truth, morality, and religious belief. The rise of digital technology and mass media has only accelerated the spread of doubt and disengagement from faith, as countless voices compete for intellectual and spiritual authority.

As we move forward, we turn to Lewis's apologetic method that masterfully integrates reason, imagination, and community—three essential dimensions of discipleship that remain as relevant today as they were in his time.

Chapter 4

C. S. Lewis's Apologetic Method

C. S. LEWIS WAS one of the most influential Christian thinkers of the twentieth century, not merely because of his ability to defend Christianity intellectually but because of the way he engaged the whole person—mind, heart, and the sense of community. His apologetic method was not a sterile intellectual exercise but a holistic approach that resonated with the deepest human longings. In an age where faith is often dismissed as outdated or irrelevant, Lewis's approach remains profoundly relevant for both evangelism and discipleship today.

Rather than relying solely on logical arguments, Lewis recognized that people are shaped by more than reason alone. He engaged the intellect through rational argumentation, the imagination through storytelling and metaphor, and the community through authentic relationships and dialogue. These three pillars—reason, imagination, and community—formed the foundation of his apologetics and offer a model for how discipleship can be revitalized in the modern world.

In this chapter, we will explore how Lewis helps us reclaim a discipleship that is both intellectually compelling and spiritually formative. First, we will examine the role of reason in establishing faith as not only credible but deeply rational, equipping believers to navigate doubts and engage thoughtfully with a skeptical world. Then, we will consider the power of imagination in awakening spiritual longing, showing how beauty, narrative, and wonder can lead people to truth in ways that mere argumentation cannot. Finally, we will reflect on the necessity of community in shaping and sustaining faith, recognizing that discipleship is not merely about knowledge but about walking together through the complexities of belief.

Through Lewis's insights, we will discover how these three elements together form a model of discipleship that does not merely inform but transforms— nourishing minds, awakening hearts, and drawing people into the fullness of life in Christ. By recovering his threefold approach, the church can equip believers to think critically, feel deeply, and grow in faith alongside others.

Discipleship and Reason

In a world where faith is often dismissed as irrational or outdated, discipleship cannot afford to ignore intellectual questions. Many people—especially young believers—encounter challenges to their faith that leave them feeling uncertain, unprepared, and vulnerable to doubt. Traditional discipleship programs often focus on biblical literacy and moral instruction but fail to address the deep philosophical and theological questions that many wrestle with. Yet, if discipleship is to be robust and transformative, it must engage both the heart and the mind.[1]

Lewis provides a model of intellectual discipleship that remains strikingly relevant today.[2] His approach to apologetics was not merely defensive—it was invitational. He did not simply argue against secularism, atheism, and relativism; he presented a vision of Christianity that was more

---

1. William Lane Craig, in *Reasonable Faith* (2008) and J.P. Moreland, in *Love Your God with All Your Mind* (2012) advocate for a renewal of Christian intellectual engagement, showing that faith is not blind but deeply rational. Charles Taylor, in *A Secular Age* (2007) explores how scientific materialism fails to answer life's deepest questions. These works affirm that faith and reason are not enemies but partners in the pursuit of truth, offering a compelling framework for overcoming the false dichotomy between faith and intellect.

2. Lewis addressed the major intellectual challenges of his time—naturalism, materialism, relativism, and skepticism—through his apologetic works, particularly in *Mere Christianity* (1952), where he argued for the rational foundation of Christian belief, and *The Abolition of Man* (1944), in which he critiqued moral relativism and the loss of objective values in modern education. In *Miracles* (1947), he directly confronted philosophical naturalism, arguing for the necessity of the supernatural, while *The Problem of Pain* (1940) tackled the challenge of suffering and theodicy. *The Screwtape Letters* (1942) and *The Great Divorce* (1945) offered imaginative critiques of secular worldviews, exposing their spiritual and moral consequences. His posthumously published *Present Concerns: Journalistic Essays* (1986) contains shorter writings addressing intellectual and cultural issues of his day.

compelling, more coherent, and more beautiful than any competing worldview. He understood that Christian faith is not a fragile belief system to be shielded from scrutiny but a reasonable and rational foundation upon which all of reality is best understood. When discipleship incorporates apologetics, it does not simply provide answers—it trains believers to think deeply, wrestle with ideas, and grow in conviction.

Lewis's Approach to Faith and Reason

Lewis was deeply committed to the idea that Christianity is not only a faith but a rational faith. He believed that reason and faith were not opposing forces but complementary aspects of the pursuit of truth. His famous statement—"I believe in Christianity as I believe that the sun has risen: not only because I see it, but because by it I see everything else"—encapsulates this conviction.[3] For Lewis, Christianity was not just a collection of religious doctrines but the very framework through which the world made sense. It was the lens that illuminated everything else, providing coherence to morality, human nature, and the deepest existential questions of life.

As a young atheist, Lewis viewed the universe as a closed system of cause and effect, governed solely by impersonal natural laws. He believed that all human thoughts, beliefs, and emotions were the byproducts of chemical and biological processes, shaped by evolutionary survival rather than by any objective truth beyond the physical world. If everything in human consciousness could be explained by material causes, then reason itself was nothing more than an adaptive function for survival—useful, perhaps, but not necessarily trustworthy in discerning reality.

However, as he began to question materialism, Lewis realized that this view of reason contained a fatal flaw. If human thought was merely the product of physical processes, determined by evolution, genetics, and neurological activity, then how could we trust it to yield objective truth? If our brains were simply wired for survival rather than truth-seeking, then there was no reason to assume that our reasoning abilities were reliable for discovering ultimate reality. This paradox—that reason itself seemed to defy naturalistic explanation—became a turning point in Lewis's intellectual journey.

In his book *Miracles*, Lewis developed a powerful argument against philosophical naturalism, often referred to as the "argument from reason."

3. Lewis, "They Asked for a Paper," 165.

He contended that if naturalism were true, then all human thoughts—including scientific discoveries, philosophical conclusions, and even arguments against Christianity—would be nothing more than material processes governed by blind physical forces. This, he argued, would undermine the very concept of rationality, as reasoning would be reduced to neuronal activity rather than objective truth-seeking. For reason to function as a trustworthy guide to reality, Lewis argued, there must be a source of rational order beyond the material world. Christianity, he maintained, provided the most coherent explanation for the existence of reason, as it posited a rational Creator who had endowed human beings with the capacity for thought, understanding, and objective knowledge.

Lewis did not merely argue that reason was compatible with faith—he insisted that reason itself pointed beyond the material world toward God. In *Mere Christianity*, he further explored the relationship between faith and reason, emphasizing that faith involves both trust and intellectual assent. He described faith as "the art of holding on to things your reason has once accepted, in spite of your changing moods."[4] Faith, for Lewis, was not a rejection of reason but a deep commitment to truth that remained steadfast even in moments of doubt and emotional turmoil. He acknowledged that human emotions and experiences fluctuate, but faith provided a rational anchor, ensuring that beliefs were not merely dictated by transient feelings.

Lewis's defense of the compatibility of faith and reason remains one of his most enduring contributions to Christian apologetics. In a time when many assumed that religion was intellectually indefensible, Lewis demonstrated that Christianity was not only reasonable, but that reason itself pointed toward a Creator. He helped skeptics recognize that faith is not a leap into the dark but a response to the light of truth, grounded in a coherent understanding of reality. His work continues to challenge the false dichotomy between faith and reason, showing that Christianity does not suppress intellectual inquiry but fulfills it. His writings remind both skeptics and believers that faith is not the opposite of reason, but rather its deepest and most profound fulfillment.

The modern world is filled with competing narratives that attempt to explain reality—secular humanism, postmodern relativism, materialistic determinism—and these narratives often present themselves as intellectually superior to religious faith. Yet, as Lewis demonstrated, they often fail to provide a coherent and livable worldview. If discipleship neglects the

---

4. Lewis, *Mere Christianity*, 125.

intellectual formation of believers, it risks leaving them vulnerable to these alternative worldviews without the tools to critically evaluate them.

The Role of Apologetics in Discipleship

Apologetics—the defense of the Christian faith—is often perceived as an intellectual pursuit reserved for scholars, theologians, and professional debaters. Many assume it belongs to the realm of academic discussions rather than the practical realities of Christian discipleship. However, Lewis demonstrated that apologetics is not an optional extra for a few well-trained individuals; it is essential for every believer. Apologetics strengthens faith, removes obstacles to belief, and prepares Christians to engage a skeptical world with confidence and clarity. Far from being a dry academic discipline, apologetics is a crucial component of spiritual formation, equipping believers to love God not only with their hearts and souls but also with their minds. Apologetics serves the church.[5]

Many modern discipleship programs emphasize personal devotion, moral living, and church involvement but neglect the intellectual formation of believers. While these aspects of discipleship are essential, ignoring the life of the mind can leave Christians ill-equipped to navigate the challenges of secularism, skepticism, and cultural relativism. This oversight is particularly dangerous in an age where atheistic and materialist worldviews dominate public discourse. Young Christians, in particular, often find themselves facing relentless assaults on their faith in academic settings, social media, and popular culture. If they have never been taught how to engage critically with competing worldviews, they may struggle to reconcile their faith with the intellectual challenges they encounter. Many find themselves questioning beliefs they once held with confidence, and some, lacking sufficient answers, ultimately drift away from the faith.

Lewis's own journey to faith illustrates why intellectual engagement must be an integral part of discipleship. As a young man, he was deeply influenced by materialist and atheistic thinkers. He initially viewed Christianity as a myth—a comforting but ultimately false narrative for those who could not face the harsh realities of an indifferent universe. For Lewis, belief in God seemed outdated, incompatible with the scientific and philosophical rigor he valued. However, as he engaged with Christian intellectuals

---

5. For a more detailed definition of apologetics, see McGrath, *Mere Apologetics* (2012); Taylor, *Introducing Apologetics* (2006); and Sproul, *Defending Your Faith* (2003).

such as Tolkien, Owen Barfield, and Chesterton, he began to recognize the philosophical inadequacy of his atheism. He saw that materialism could not account for the very things that mattered most to him: the existence of reason, the objectivity of moral values, and the universal human longing for something beyond the material world.

One of the most pivotal moments in Lewis's journey came when he realized that his deep longing for meaning, beauty, and truth was not an illusion but a signpost pointing toward the reality of God. He recognized that his love for great literature, his awe at the beauty of the natural world, and his desire for something beyond what this world could offer were not meaningless coincidences. Rather, they were indications that he was made for something more. He later described this realization as an intellectual awakening—one that led him to see Christianity not as a mere religious tradition but as the key that unlocked the mystery of human experience.

This understanding profoundly shaped Lewis's approach to evangelism and discipleship. He did not engage in apologetics merely to win arguments or silence critics. Instead, he sought to awaken people to the truth of Christianity in a way that resonated with their deepest experiences. His method combined rigorous logic with profound existential insight. He invited skeptics not just to consider whether Christianity was true in a theoretical sense but whether it explained the world, human nature, and the longings of the human heart better than any alternative. This is why Lewis's apologetics were so effective: he addressed both the intellectual and the existential dimensions of belief, appealing to the mind and the imagination, to reason and to longing.

The integration of apologetics into discipleship is not only a reflection of Lewis's approach but is also deeply rooted in Scripture. The Bible consistently affirms the importance of reasoned faith and intellectual engagement. Peter's exhortation to "always be prepared to give an answer to everyone who asks you to give the reason for the hope that you have" (1 Pet 3:15) highlights the responsibility of every believer to be ready to articulate the reasons for their faith. Jesus's command to "love the Lord your God with all your heart and with all your soul and with all your mind" (Matt 22:37) makes it clear that Christian discipleship involves not just spiritual devotion but intellectual engagement. It involves learning how to love God with our minds. Paul's speech at the Areopagus in Acts 17 demonstrates an apologetic approach tailored to a skeptical audience. He does not merely proclaim the gospel but reasons with the philosophers of Athens, appealing to their own beliefs and cultural references. Even in the Old Testament, God himself invites his people to "reason together" with him (Isa 1:18), affirming that faith and reason are not opposed but are meant to work together.

This model of apologetics offers profound implications for discipleship today. The church must recognize that believers—especially young people—are constantly engaging with ideas that challenge their faith. Whether they encounter them in university classrooms, workplace discussions, social media debates, or casual conversations, they need to be equipped to respond with wisdom and confidence. Intellectual doubt does not have to lead to a crisis of faith if believers have been trained to think critically and wrestle honestly with difficult questions. Apologetics must not be treated as an occasional topic within discipleship but as an essential part of spiritual formation.

Timothy Keller echoes this necessity in *The Reason for God*, where he emphasizes that many people walk away from Christianity not because they have been argued out of it but because they have never been given the space to voice their questions. He writes, "A faith without some doubts is like a human body without any antibodies in it."[6] If believers are not given opportunities to explore their doubts in a safe and constructive way, they will be vulnerable to secular ideologies that offer seemingly compelling alternatives.

Beyond formal instruction, apologetics should be woven into the fabric of discipleship relationships. Mature believers should mentor younger Christians, not only teaching them biblical truths but helping them engage with real-world challenges to their faith. Just as Lewis was influenced by personal conversations with intellectually rigorous Christians, believers today benefit from relationships where they can openly discuss doubts, questions, and the intellectual aspects of their faith journey. A culture of discipleship that encourages critical thinking will produce mature Christians who are not easily shaken when confronted with opposing worldviews.

However, it is crucial that apologetics in discipleship does not become a mere exercise in intellectual superiority or debate-winning. The goal is not to equip believers with rhetorical weapons to defeat their opponents but to cultivate a love for truth and a compassionate approach to dialogue. Lewis exemplified this by treating his intellectual opponents with respect and humility. He understood that apologetics is most effective when it is not simply about defending Christianity but about inviting people into a

---

6. Keller, *The Reason for God*, xxiii.

fuller understanding of reality. This means that apologetics must always be conducted with both confidence and gentleness, offering compelling arguments while also demonstrating the character of Christ.

Apologetics in discipleship, therefore, is not about creating intellectual superiority or merely winning debates—it is about strengthening faith, removing obstacles to belief, and leading people into a deeper relationship with Christ. The Christian faith is not blind; it is deeply rational, coherent, and satisfying. When believers see that Christianity is not only emotionally fulfilling but intellectually credible, they are better equipped to stand firm, to share the gospel, and to live out their calling in a world that desperately needs the light of Christ.

Faith Seeking Understanding

Lewis exemplified the idea that discipleship involves faith seeking understanding, a concept rooted in the early church and championed by theologians such as Augustine and Anselm. In other words, Christianity not only explains the world better than any competing worldview but also resonates deeply with the longings of the human heart.

Scripture never presents faith as irrational or anti-intellectual; rather, it calls believers to seek wisdom and understanding. Proverbs 2:3-6 urges, "Indeed, if you call out for insight and cry aloud for understanding . . . then you will understand the fear of the LORD and find the knowledge of God. For the LORD gives wisdom; from His mouth come knowledge and understanding." Faith is meant to engage the mind, and discipleship must reflect this by equipping believers to think deeply about what they believe and why.

Anselm of Canterbury famously described faith as *fides quaerens intellectum*—faith seeking understanding.[7] He believed that faith is not static but grows through reflection, questioning, and deep engagement with reality. This is precisely what Lewis sought to model. He did not reduce faith to an abstract intellectual exercise, nor did he dismiss reason in favor of mere personal experience. Instead, he integrated both, showing that faith is reasonable but also beautiful, that it makes sense but also awakens desire. He invited his readers into a discipleship that was both intellectually compelling and existentially rich, allowing them to see Christianity not just as true but as wonderfully true.

7. Anselm, *Proslogion* (1965).

This integration of faith and reason is essential in a world where Christianity is often viewed as intellectually untenable, outdated, or even oppressive. The secular narrative presents reason and faith as incompatible, forcing many believers into an unnecessary and false dichotomy. Many young Christians grow up in churches where discipleship focuses on superficial personal devotion and moral instruction but offers little intellectual engagement. When these believers later encounter challenges to their faith in academic settings, online debates, or even casual conversations, they often feel unprepared. Without a framework for understanding how faith relates to reason, history, and science, many struggle in silence. Some assume that their faith is opposed to intellectual inquiry and either retreat into an anti-intellectual stance or walk away from Christianity altogether.

The biblical call to discipleship includes a call to grow in knowledge and understanding. It also includes a call to love God with our minds. In Colossians 2:2–3, Paul prays that believers would "reach all the riches of full assurance of understanding and the knowledge of God's mystery, which is Christ, in whom are hidden all the treasures of wisdom and knowledge." Faith is not static; it matures through seeking wisdom and aligning one's thinking with divine truth. An unexamined faith is vulnerable, easily shaken by intellectual challenges or personal trials. Therefore, true discipleship must encourage believers to engage with the deepest questions of life—not out of fear that their faith will collapse, but with the confidence that truth will always lead them closer to God.

The process of faith seeking understanding also reflects the biblical pattern of growth in discipleship. In 2 Peter 1:5–6, believers are instructed to "make every effort to supplement your faith with virtue, and virtue with knowledge." The Christian life involves an active pursuit of truth, where faith is strengthened through disciplined study and reflection. Lewis exemplified this in his own journey. Though he was initially drawn to Christianity through reason, his faith deepened as he continued to explore its implications in every aspect of life. His commitment to learning was not limited to apologetics but extended into literature, philosophy, and the arts, demonstrating that a robust faith embraces intellectual curiosity rather than retreating from it.

Many Christians struggle when confronted with secular ideologies that claim to offer a more sophisticated, enlightened view of reality. Without a framework for understanding the coherence of Christianity, they may feel pressured to conform to the prevailing intellectual trends of the culture. Discipleship must, therefore, provide believers with the tools to analyze worldviews critically, to discern truth from error, and to apply biblical wisdom to contemporary issues. This does not mean turning faith into an intellectual exercise detached from daily life; rather, it means forming disciples who can engage with confidence, knowing that the Christian faith is not only spiritually fulfilling but intellectually satisfying.

Moreover, Lewis recognized that faith seeking understanding is not merely about answering external challenges—it is also about deepening personal conviction. Too often, doubt is stigmatized in Christian communities, leaving those with honest struggles feeling isolated. However, Scripture shows that questioning can be part of a faithful pursuit of truth. In Mark 9:24, the father of the demon-possessed boy cries out, "I believe; help my unbelief!" This tension between faith and doubt is common in the Christian journey, and Lewis himself experienced it at various points in his life. He did not see doubt as the enemy of faith but as an opportunity for deeper understanding and greater assurance.

Lewis's legacy reminds us that the best discipleship is one that leads believers into a fuller understanding of reality—one that strengthens their confidence in the truth of Christianity, equips them to address difficult questions, and deepens their love for God. In a world filled with competing philosophies and distractions, this kind of discipleship is not just desirable—it is essential.

However, while reason is essential to discipleship, Lewis recognized that people are not won over by logic alone. The imagination plays a crucial role in shaping our understanding of reality. Through storytelling, metaphor, and beauty, Lewis invited people to experience the truth of Christianity in a way that resonated deeply with their hearts. How can we use imagination in discipleship to awaken spiritual longing?

Discipleship and Imagination

In a post-Christian age, many people are not rejecting Christianity because they have carefully examined its claims and found them wanting. Rather, they are indifferent to it. Christianity does not seem necessary, relevant, or even particularly interesting. People are so preoccupied with their immediate desires and distractions that they rarely stop to ask the bigger questions of life. They do not reject God outright—they simply do not feel his absence. For this reason, discipleship must not only engage the intellect—it must capture the heart.

Lewis understood that before people accept Christianity as true, they must first desire it to be true. He recognized that human beings are not merely rational creatures but deeply imaginative ones. The deepest longing of the human heart, he believed, is for something beyond this world—something that transcends the mundane, the temporary, and the ordinary. This longing manifests in moments of wonder, beauty, and profound joy—what he famously called "Joy" with a capital J—an intense yearning for something we cannot quite name. Lewis saw beauty, imagination, and storytelling as powerful tools for awakening this longing and pointing people toward its ultimate fulfillment in God.

Lewis's use of *sehnsucht*—a German word that roughly translates as "longing" or "yearning"—captures a central theme in both his personal spiritual journey and his vision of Christian discipleship.[8] For Lewis, *sehnsucht* was not merely a passing emotion, but a profound existential experience: a deep, unshakable yearning for something beyond the reach of this world. He often referred to it as an "inconsolable secret" within each person—an ache for a joy that seems just out of reach, a desire for a place or reality we've never seen, yet feel we somehow remember. This sense of longing haunted him from childhood, surfacing in moments of beauty, music, nature, or literature—what he called "drops of joy" that were intense, fleeting, and ultimately unsatisfying in themselves, yet hinted at something greater beyond them.

In his autobiographical work *Surprised by Joy*, Lewis describes how these moments of *sehnsucht* played a key role in awakening him to the presence of God. Initially, he chased the feeling itself—trying to reproduce the emotion through repeated exposure to music, poetry, or nature—but he eventually realized that the longing was not the object of desire, but a signpost pointing beyond the material to the eternal. The longing, in other words, was not a defect or illusion to be dismissed, but a *clue*—an arrow directing his heart toward the source of all joy and beauty: God himself.

In this light, *sehnsucht* becomes not just a psychological curiosity but a theological insight. Lewis came to see that this deep longing was implanted by God as a kind of homing instinct, meant to draw the soul upward and outward toward its true home. It is a longing that no earthly

---

8. Lewis uses the term *sehnsucht* throughout his writings to describe a deep, inconsolable longing for something beyond this world. See Lewis, *The Weight of Glory*, 4-5.

pleasure can fulfill, precisely because it is a desire for the infinite—for the divine. And because the imagination is often the faculty through which this longing is awakened, Lewis saw it as essential to discipleship. Imagination doesn't lead us away from truth, but prepares the heart to *recognize* truth when it comes. Through story, symbol, and beauty, Lewis invited his readers not merely to believe in God, but to *desire* him—to feel the pull of eternity, to be stirred by joy, and to recognize that the longing within them was not something to be satisfied by this world, but by the God who made them and who calls them home.

Unlike many modern thinkers, who often reduce Christianity to a system of ethics or a series of intellectual propositions, Lewis understood that faith is more than just a set of doctrines—it is an invitation into a larger story. The Christian faith is not merely a collection of rules and beliefs; it is a breathtaking narrative of creation, fall, redemption, and restoration. It is the story that gives meaning to all other stories. Lewis used myth, metaphor, and wonder to make this grand narrative come alive, allowing people to feel the weight of sin, the joy of redemption, and the hope of heaven.

This approach is perhaps most vividly displayed in *Ransom Trilogy—Out of the Silent Planet*, *Perelandra*, and *That Hideous Strength*. Unlike his theological essays, these novels do not argue for Christianity in a direct, propositional manner. Instead, they immerse the reader in a world where spiritual realities are made tangible.

In *Out of the Silent Planet* (1938), Lewis presents a vision of an unfallen world, Malacandra (Mars), where creatures live in harmony with divine order. By contrasting this world with Earth—bent and corrupted by sin—Lewis compels readers to see their own world anew. The novel reawakens a sense of wonder, stripping away the assumption that sin is normal and showing that life in submission to God is not oppressive but liberating.

In *Perelandra* (1943), Lewis goes further, exploring a new Eden (Venus), where Ransom encounters an unfallen woman facing temptation. The antagonist, Weston—now an agent of diabolical influence—does not simply present falsehoods; he weaves compelling narratives to deceive. This imaginative depiction of temptation shows that evil often persuades through stories, not just arguments. Discipleship in a post-Christian age must recognize this reality: people are not merely convinced by logic; they are captivated by the narratives they embrace. The church, then, must not only teach truth but present a vision of life in Christ that is more compelling than the secular myths that dominate modern culture.

The final novel, *That Hideous Strength* (1945), shifts from cosmic adventure to an Earth-bound dystopia, where a totalitarian organization, N.I.C.E., seeks to control human destiny through science and technocratic power. Here, Lewis critiques a world that has lost its imagination—a world that sees only raw material to be manipulated rather than a creation infused with meaning. In contrast, the small, hidden community at St. Anne's represents a vision of true discipleship: a fellowship bound not by power but by faithfulness to a higher reality. In our disenchanted age, where meaning is often reduced to material progress, *That Hideous Strength* serves as a prophetic warning and a call to reclaim the imagination as essential to Christian life.

Therefore, the use of imagination can shape a discipleship model that does more than just inform the mind—it awakens the soul. By recovering the role of imagination in discipleship, the church can stir spiritual hunger in an apathetic world, drawing people toward the deep joy and fulfillment that only Christ can provide.

Imagination as a Pathway to Truth

Lewis's journey to faith was not merely an intellectual pursuit—it was profoundly shaped by the power of imagination. As a young atheist, he was steeped in materialist and rationalist philosophy, convinced that religious belief was nothing more than an outdated superstition, a psychological crutch for those unwilling to accept the cold, impersonal nature of the universe. He had absorbed the skepticism of thinkers such as H. G. Wells, Bertrand Russell, and Sigmund Freud, who regarded faith as a projection of human desires rather than a response to objective truth. To Lewis, Christianity seemed no different from the myths of ancient civilizations—stories that once provided meaning but had long since been replaced by the enlightenment of reason and scientific progress.

Yet, even as Lewis rejected Christianity on an intellectual level, he found himself continually haunted by something deeper—an inexplicable longing that he could not ignore.

At first, Lewis believed that these moments were nothing more than aesthetic or psychological reactions. He tried to recapture them through literature, music, and philosophy, but they always faded, leaving behind a sense of longing rather than fulfillment. Over time, he realized that these experiences were not ends in themselves but signposts—clues embedded in the fabric of existence, pointing to a greater reality. In *Mere Christianity*, he described how he came to see that these desires were not illusions but evidence that he was made for something beyond the natural world. He famously wrote: "Creatures are not born with desires unless satisfaction for those desires exists. A baby feels hunger: well, there is such a thing as food. A duckling wants to swim: well, there is such a thing as water. Men feel sexual desire: well, there is such a thing as sex. If I find in myself a desire which no experience in this world can satisfy, the most probable explanation is that I was made for another world."[9]

Lewis understood that, while logical arguments might convince people of Christianity's intellectual credibility, it was often imagination that first awakened them to its desirability. People do not merely want to know that God exists—they want to see him, to experience his beauty, to feel the weight of his glory. Lewis grasped that faith was not merely a matter of intellectual assent but of seeing reality rightly. His goal was not simply to prove that Christianity was true but to help people realize that they had always known it to be true in the deepest recesses of their hearts.

The Bible itself affirms the role of imagination in shaping faith. Scripture does not merely present a set of theological propositions—it tells a story. From Genesis to Revelation, God reveals himself through narratives, poetry, visions, and parables. Jesus, the ultimate teacher, did not lecture his disciples with abstract philosophical arguments; he told stories. He spoke of a father running to embrace his prodigal son, a shepherd searching for a lost sheep, a mustard seed growing into a mighty tree. He used imagery that stirred the imagination, inviting his listeners to see the kingdom of God rather than just understand it. Faith is not just about knowledge—it is about perceiving reality through the lens of divine truth.

Lewis's recognition of imagination as a pathway to truth was rooted in his belief that modernity had stripped reality of its enchantment. The materialist worldview, which dominated his early intellectual life, had reduced the world to mere physical processes, stripping it of meaning, purpose, and wonder. Science, while valuable in describing how things work, could not explain why they exist in the first place. In contrast, Lewis argued that imagination allows us to see the world as it truly is—not as a cold, mechanistic system, but as a creation infused with divine purpose.

Kevin Vanhoozer has long emphasized that theology is not merely about acquiring knowledge but about learning to see and live within the

---

9. Lewis, *Mere Christianity*, 120-21.

drama of redemption. In *Faith Speaking Understanding*, he argues that Christian discipleship is a matter of participation in God's unfolding story, not just intellectual assent to doctrinal truths. He describes theology as "theodramatic" engagement, where believers inhabit the biblical narrative and embody its truths in their lives. This resonates deeply with Lewis's conviction that faith is not merely a rational system but a way of perceiving and living in reality rightly. Christianity is not an abstract ideology but a story that demands participation, shaping both the imagination and the affections of believers.[10]

Vanhoozer also critiques modern secularism for reducing the world to mere facts, stripping it of meaning and transcendence. In *Pictures at a Theological Exhibition*, he argues that imagination is crucial for resisting this disenchantment and recovering a fully Christian vision of the world.[11] Like Lewis, Vanhoozer sees the imagination not as an escape from reality but as a means of perceiving its deepest truths. He describes biblical doctrine not merely as a set of propositions but as a script for life, inviting believers to play their part in the grand drama of redemption. This reinforces Lewis's conviction that faith is not just about knowing the right answers but about stepping into the story of God's kingdom. If modern culture suffers from spiritual apathy, the solution is not only intellectual engagement but also an imaginative reawakening—one that rekindles a sense of wonder and awe. Vanhoozer's insights remind us that the church must reclaim the beauty of biblical narrative, worship, and the arts to present Christianity not merely as an argument to be accepted but as a reality to be embraced, lived, and loved. In other words, if people are to be drawn to faith, they must first desire it to be true. Before they accept Christianity, they must first want it.

If we recognize that one of the greatest challenges facing the church today is not merely intellectual skepticism but spiritual apathy, then we must also understand the vital role of imagination in discipleship. Rational arguments, while essential, are not enough on their own—people must first perceive the beauty of the gospel before they will desire its truth. Too often, churches reduce faith to a set of doctrines to be memorized rather than a reality to be encountered. Discipleship becomes a program rather than an adventure. But faith cannot thrive in a purely rationalistic framework—it must be felt, seen, experienced. This is why Scripture calls us not only to know God but to taste and see that the Lord is good (Ps 34:8).

10. Vanhoozer, *Faith Speaking Understanding*, 3-5.
11. Vanhoozer, *Pictures at a Theological Exhibition*, 23-25.

Lewis's legacy reminds us that imagination is not the enemy of faith—it is one of its greatest allies. By awakening desire, breaking through indifference, and revealing glimpses of divine truth, imagination has the power to stir the soul toward God. In a world that has forgotten what it is longing for, the church must once again become a place where wonder is cultivated, where beauty is celebrated, and where faith is not merely taught but seen, felt, and lived.

The Power of Storytelling in Discipleship

Lewis understood that storytelling is not simply a tool for entertainment; it is a means of revealing truth. Unlike abstract theological discourse, which appeals primarily to the intellect, stories engage both the mind and the heart, drawing readers into an experience rather than simply presenting them with information. Lewis once distinguished reason and imagination by calling reason the natural *organ of truth* and imagination the *organ of meaning*. While reason dissects and analyzes, imagination synthesizes and perceives, enabling us to grasp reality in a way that logic alone cannot. Jesus modeled this method of teaching through His parables, using simple yet profound stories to illuminate deep spiritual truths. When Jesus spoke of a father running to embrace a prodigal son (Luke 15:11–32), a man discovering a treasure hidden in a field (Matt 13:44), or a vineyard owner extending radical grace to his workers (Matt 20:1–16), he was not merely communicating doctrine—he was helping his listeners see the kingdom of God in ways that logic alone could not convey.

Lewis, in following this tradition, recognized that people are often resistant to truth when it is presented in purely propositional form. However, when that same truth is woven into a compelling narrative, it bypasses intellectual defenses and speaks directly to the soul. This is why his most enduring works are not his explicitly theological writings but his works of fiction—*The Chronicles of Narnia*, *Ransom Trilogy*, and *The Great Divorce*. Through these stories, Lewis was able to illuminate deep theological realities in ways that made them both understandable and deeply moving.

Great stories do more than inform—they transform. They have the ability to stir emotions, awaken longing, and invite readers into an encounter with truth that is felt as much as it is understood. A theological lecture on the atonement might explain the mechanics of substitutionary sacrifice, but experiencing Aslan willingly offering his life on the Stone Table in *The Lion, the*

Witch, and the Wardrobe makes that truth tangible. Readers do not merely learn about sacrificial love; they feel it. The weight of Edmund's betrayal, the horror of Aslan's humiliation, and the joy of his resurrection create an emotional experience that lingers long after the book is closed.

The Bible itself is a grand narrative, unfolding the story of creation, fall, redemption, and restoration. It is not structured as a systematic theology textbook but as a sweeping epic of God's interaction with humanity. From the opening chapters of Genesis, where God speaks creation into existence, to the climactic visions of Revelation, where he restores all things, the Bible tells a story that captures both the imagination and the intellect. The gospel is not merely a collection of doctrines—it is the greatest story ever told.

Lewis understood this better than most. He saw that human beings are wired for stories, that we instinctively seek meaning in narrative form. He believed that the myths and legends of human history—tales of dying and rising gods, of sacrificial heroes, of good triumphing over evil—were not mere fabrications but echoes of the ultimate truth found in Christ. The gospel is the fulfillment of all myths, the moment when the grand story humanity has always longed for became real in history. Christianity, according to Lewis, "is precisely the story of the true God expressing himself through what we call 'real things'—namely, the actual incarnation, crucifixion, and resurrection."[12]

This insight shaped not only Lewis's apologetics but his approach to discipleship. The modern, secular mindset tends to view reality as disenchanted, reducing existence to mere material processes. But Lewis sought to reawaken his readers to the wonder and mystery of reality, to help them see that they live in a world brimming with divine presence. Through his fiction, he invited them to step into that enchanted vision—to see that the world is not a cold, meaningless machine but a story written by the Author of life himself.

One of the most striking examples of how Lewis uses storytelling to communicate deep spiritual truths is found in *The Great Divorce*, his imaginative exploration of heaven, hell, and the choices that shape human destiny. Instead of offering a philosophical treatise on the nature of salvation, Lewis presents a dreamlike journey where ghosts from hell are given the opportunity to enter heaven—but most of them refuse. They cling to

---

12. Lewis in a letter to Arthur Greeves: from The Kilns (on his conversion to Christianity), 18 October 1931.

their pride, their bitterness, their illusions of self-sufficiency, even when confronted with the overwhelming joy of God's presence. Lewis forces readers to confront their own tendencies toward sin and self-deception, not through direct argumentation but through an encounter with vivid, unforgettable characters. The man who clings to his pet sins, the woman who cannot let go of her self-pity, the intellectual who prefers abstract speculation to divine reality—all of them reflect the choices that every person must face. By presenting these ideas in a story rather than a lecture, Lewis makes them deeply personal, prompting readers to examine their own hearts in ways that a theological essay might not.

This is the power of imaginative discipleship. It allows people to experience truth rather than merely being told about it. It engages not only the mind but the emotions, awakening a longing for the divine that cannot be reduced to mere intellectual agreement.

Recovering the Role of Imagination in the Church

The modern church has often neglected the power of imagination in discipleship, favoring analytical approaches to faith while leaving behind the rich, transformative potential of beauty, wonder, and creativity. Sermons, Bible studies, and Christian education tend to focus heavily on systematic theology, biblical exposition, and moral instruction. While these elements are essential for a well-grounded faith, they are not enough on their own. A faith that only instructs but does not inspire will struggle to capture hearts, and a discipleship model that focuses solely on intellectual comprehension risks leaving the soul unstirred.

Throughout history, Christian faith has flourished when it has engaged the imagination alongside reason. The medieval cathedrals, illuminated manuscripts, stained-glass windows, and epic poetry of Dante and Milton were not merely decorative—they were acts of theological vision, inviting worshippers to step into a world infused with divine meaning. Even the earliest Christian communities were marked by storytelling, hymns, and acts that reinforced spiritual truths. The modern church must reclaim this heritage, recognizing that imagination is not a distraction from truth but a pathway into it.

To cultivate a discipleship model that engages the imagination, the church must once again embrace creativity and storytelling. Worship should not be merely an intellectual exercise but a visceral experience of God's glory. Music, poetry, and visual art should be integrated into discipleship, allowing believers to experience the depth of God's presence beyond mere words. When worship is stripped of beauty and mystery, it risks becoming dry and mechanical. But when it engages the whole person—mind, heart, and senses—it has the power to draw believers into an encounter with the living God.

Sermons and teaching should also be shaped by the power of metaphor, parable, and imagery—just as Jesus taught. When Jesus spoke of the kingdom of God, he did not deliver dry theological lectures; he told stories. He painted pictures with words, describing a father running to embrace a prodigal son, a shepherd searching for a lost sheep, a tiny mustard seed growing into a mighty tree. When Paul preached, it was as if he were portraying Christ crucified so that the church could see him (Gal 3:1). These images linger in the mind long after doctrinal statements fade. The church must recover this kind of preaching and teaching, using stories, illustrations, and symbolic language to illuminate theological truths in ways that engage both the intellect and the heart.

Beyond sermons, the church must actively encourage believers to engage individually and in small groups with literature and art that stirs the soul. Christian imagination should not be confined to explicitly religious works; rather, believers should be trained to recognize God's truth wherever it appears. Great stories—whether *The Chronicles of Narnia*, *The Lord of the Rings*, or *The Brothers Karamazov*—offer glimpses of redemption, sacrifice, and grace. They help believers develop a theological imagination that sees the world as infused with meaning, shaped by a divine narrative. Discipleship should foster book clubs and discussions that deepen faith through creativity, showing how all beauty ultimately reflects the Creator.

The beauty of creation itself should also be emphasized as a source of discipleship (Psalm 19). In our technologically driven world, many people have lost the ability to see—to behold the grandeur of a sunrise, the delicate intricacy of a flower, the majesty of the stars. God's artistry is on display in the natural world, yet modern life often blinds us to its significance. Discipleship should include practices that cultivate attentiveness to beauty as a means of spiritual formation. Time spent in nature, whether through hiking, gardening, or simply sitting in silence, can awaken a sense of awe and draw people into deeper communion with God.

Furthermore, the church must recognize that imagination is not only awakened by what we see but by what we experience. In an age of constant distraction, many people have lost the ability to engage deeply with anything. Social media, entertainment, and endless noise have dulled our capacity for wonder, leaving us restless yet unable to satisfy the deeper hunger within us. Discipleship must therefore include intentional practices that cultivate stillness, reflection, and contemplation. Silent retreats, liturgical rhythms, and ancient disciplines such as *lectio divina* and contemplative prayer can help reawaken this sense of wonder, creating space for God to speak to the imagination.

When the imagination is cultivated in discipleship, faith becomes something more than just an obligation—it becomes an invitation. People are no longer merely told what to believe; they are drawn into the why of belief. They begin to see the world not as a random collection of events but as a meaningful, unfolding story in which they have a role to play. Christianity is not merely a set of doctrines; it is the true myth, as Lewis put it—the one story that explains all other stories. When believers see their own lives as part of this grand narrative, their faith is no longer just an intellectual exercise but a lived, imaginative, and deeply transformative reality.

However, the Christian faith was never meant to be lived in isolation. Just as imagination helps awaken desire for truth, community is essential for sustaining and nurturing faith. Lewis himself thrived in the company of close friends who sharpened his thinking and encouraged his spiritual growth. The church today must rediscover the power of relationships in forming disciples who remain faithful and fruitful.

Discipleship and Community

Discipleship is not merely about acquiring knowledge or engaging the imagination—it is about sharing life in a community shaped by the gospel. In the early church, discipleship was not a structured program but a lived reality, woven into the fabric of daily relationships. Believers grew in faith by walking alongside one another, encouraging, supporting, and challenging each other in love. Christianity spread not through detached religious instruction but through deep, personal connections where the truth of the gospel was not only taught but embodied. True discipleship is not just the transmission of doctrine; it is the formation of a people whose lives bear witness to the transforming power of Christ.

C. S. Lewis, in *Out of the Silent Planet*, emphasizes this when he writes, "What we need for the moment is not so much a body of belief as a body of people familiarized with certain ideas."[13] In context, Lewis is addressing the way ideas take root and shape a culture—not through abstract arguments alone but through a living community that breathes and exemplifies those ideas. This is crucial for discipleship in a post-Christian age, where Christian truths are often dismissed or ignored, not because they have been thoroughly refuted, but because they are no longer culturally embodied. If people are to grasp the reality of God's kingdom, they must see it in action—through a church that models grace, truth, and love in tangible ways. This was Lesslie Newbigin's understanding when he wrote, "since the gospel does not come as a disembodied message, but as the message of a community which claims to live by it and which invites others to adhere to it, the community's life must be so ordered that it 'makes sense' to those who are so invited."[14]

Lewis and Newbigin converge in their conviction that truth must be incarnated in community. While Lewis focuses on the cultural formation that occurs through familiarization with ideas lived out in a community, Newbigin presses this further by asserting that the credibility of the gospel itself is bound to the plausibility of the church's witness. For both thinkers, the church is not merely a container for doctrine but the very medium through which the message of the gospel is made visible and believable. In a fragmented digital age where abstract claims are easily dismissed, the lived coherence of a gospel-shaped community becomes an apologetic in itself—a "plausibility structure," as Newbigin might say, that allows the message of Christ to be heard afresh.[15]

This understanding is vital because it frames the church not merely as a dispenser of religious information but as a living, breathing community in which the truth of the gospel is made tangible. In a society where individual autonomy and curated online identities dominate, the church offers a radically different vision of life—one rooted in mutual dependence, vulnerability, and shared purpose. When Christians embody the gospel in

---

13. Lewis, *Out of the Silent Planet*, 167.

14. Newbigin, *The Gospel in a Pluralist Society*, 141.

15. The term *plausibility structure* refers to the sociological concept popularized by Peter Berger and adopted by Lesslie Newbigin to describe the social and communal context in which certain beliefs are considered credible or believable. For Newbigin, the church is called to be a countercultural community that embodies the gospel in such a way that it provides a new plausibility structure—one in which the claims of Christianity make sense and can be seen as both reasonable and livable in contrast to the dominant cultural narratives. See Lesslie Newbigin, *The Gospel in a Pluralist Society*, 1989.

their relationships, practices, and communal life, they create a plausibility structure in which discipleship becomes both credible and compelling. The community doesn't just transmit doctrine; it demonstrates what it means to belong to Christ and live under His lordship.

Moreover, discipleship detached from authentic community risks becoming either abstract or performative. It may foster intellectual agreement without transformation, or personal piety without accountability. But when believers engage in life together—confessing sin, bearing burdens, rejoicing and mourning as one body—they participate in a formative environment where growth in Christ becomes a shared journey. This is the kind of community Lewis envisioned and Newbigin insisted upon: one where the gospel makes sense because it is seen, not just heard. In the digital age, where isolation and skepticism often prevail, such embodied witness is not optional—it is essential.

Lewis understood this deeply. Though he was an academic and a brilliant writer, he was also profoundly relational. He knew that faith is not merely taught—it is shared, cultivated, and nurtured within the context of relationships. He did not treat skeptics with arrogance or dismiss their doubts—he met them where they were, engaged their concerns with patience, and shared his own struggles. Whether through his letters, friendships, or writings, Lewis exemplified the idea that discipleship happens best in the context of genuine relationships.

Lewis and the Art of Engaging with Others

Though he was a distinguished professor at Oxford and later at Cambridge, Lewis did not allow the walls of academia to isolate him from ordinary seekers, skeptics, and fellow believers. Unlike many intellectuals who preferred to remain within the world of abstract debates and scholarly discussions, Lewis made it a priority to connect with people at a deeply personal level. He welcomed dialogue, treating the struggles, doubts, and inquiries of others with respect and sincerity. His approach was not to overpower with arguments but to patiently walk with people as they explored the claims of Christianity.

This deep engagement was perhaps most evident in his prolific correspondence. Throughout his life, Lewis wrote thousands of letters to people from around the world—students, soldiers, pastors, skeptics, and ordinary men and women seeking guidance in their faith. His letters reveal a man who did not dismiss the doubts of atheists or agnostics as trivial but took their concerns seriously. He responded not only with intellectual rigor but also with warmth and encouragement, demonstrating that he saw faith not merely as a set of doctrines to be defended but as a lived reality to be nurtured through conversation and reflection.

His approach was deeply relational, reflecting the biblical model of discipleship. In the New Testament, we see that Jesus did not merely teach in public but engaged personally with individuals—Nicodemus the Pharisee (John 3), the Samaritan woman at the well (John 4), and Thomas the doubter (John 20:24–29). Jesus welcomed questions, addressed doubts, and treated each person with both truth and compassion. Lewis followed this same model, believing that faith was best explored not through one-sided instruction but through honest and open dialogue.

One of the most significant examples of Lewis's relational approach to discipleship was his involvement in the *Inklings*, a group of writers, scholars, and Christian thinkers who met regularly to discuss literature, theology, and philosophy. The *Inklings* did not simply exchange academic ideas; they shared their struggles, encouraged one another, and refined each other's thoughts through discussion and critique. These meetings were not impersonal lectures but lively, engaged conversations where truth was sharpened through friendship. Tolkien captured the essence of their fellowship with simple yet profound enthusiasm, exclaiming, "That was true joy!" Lewis, reflecting on the richness of their gatherings, mused, "Is any pleasure on earth as great as a circle of Christian friends by a good fire?" He later acknowledged the immeasurable impact of these friendships, remarking, "What I owe to them all is incalculable."[16]

This model of discipleship, rooted in real relationships and mutual encouragement, provides an important lesson for the church today. Too often, discipleship is reduced to one-way instruction, where information is passed down without genuine dialogue. Many churches structure discipleship programs around curriculum-driven courses that do not allow space for questions, doubts, or deep discussion. Yet, Lewis's life and ministry remind us that faith grows best in the context of authentic relationships. His friendships with Tolkien and others played a vital role in deepening his understanding of Christianity, shaping his theological imagination, and refining his ability to articulate the faith. He was not a solitary thinker; his

---

16. Lewis, *The Collected Letters of C. S. Lewis*, Volume 2 (To Dom Bede Griffiths on December 21, 1941).

convictions were tested, strengthened, and clarified in ongoing conversations with others who shared his love for truth.

This emphasis on dialogue and relationship is evident in the early church as well. The apostle Paul's letters, for example, are not abstract theological treatises but deeply personal messages to communities of believers with whom he had real relationships. He encouraged believers to "teach and admonish one another in all wisdom" (Col 3:16), to "speak the truth in love" (Eph 4:15), and to "bear one another's burdens" (Gal 6:2). Discipleship in the early church was a communal process, a shared journey of growing together in faith, not merely an academic exercise or an isolated pursuit.

The church today can learn from this by fostering environments where discipleship is not just about imparting knowledge but about cultivating trust, friendship, and shared discovery. Many believers, particularly those struggling with doubts or past wounds, need safe spaces where they can express their uncertainties without fear of judgment, where they can be met with patience rather than quick, rehearsed answers, and where they can explore faith as part of a shared journey.

In a world that often prioritizes efficiency and mass communication over deep personal connection, we need to recover the lost art of engaging in meaningful spiritual conversations. Discipleship is not about downloading information into someone's mind—it is about walking with them in love, as Christ walked with His disciples. Jesus modeled this by spending time with his followers, answering their questions, correcting them with patience, and revealing truth through lived experience. True discipleship requires an investment in relationships, a willingness to listen, and the humility to engage with people where they are rather than where we expect them to be.

Lewis's willingness to engage personally with those who had questions about Christianity reflects an approach to discipleship that prioritizes relationship over argument. He understood that conversion is rarely the result of a single debate or a perfectly crafted argument; rather, it often happens in the context of trust, where an individual feels safe to explore faith without pressure or condemnation. The goal of discipleship, then, is not simply to equip people with apologetic answers but to walk with them as they grow in understanding and trust.

C. S. LEWIS'S APOLOGETIC METHOD

Empathy as the Foundation for Discipleship

At the heart of Lewis's approach to engaging with others was empathy. He understood that many who struggled with faith were not simply rebellious or intellectually dishonest; they were often wounded, confused, or carrying deep doubts they did not know how to resolve. Rather than dismissing their skepticism as a sign of defiance, he saw it as an expression of their personal experiences—pain, loss, disappointment, or a sense of alienation from the idea of a loving God. Lewis's own life bore the marks of suffering and doubt. Losing his mother at a young age, enduring the horrors of World War I, and wrestling through a long period of atheism gave him a unique ability to sympathize with those who questioned the existence or goodness of God. He knew firsthand what it was like to stand on the precipice of belief, longing for truth but held back by suffering and uncertainty.

This deep personal experience of pain and searching shaped his entire approach to apologetics and discipleship. Unlike those who dismiss doubt as mere stubbornness or intellectual pride, Lewis saw it as part of the human condition—something to be addressed with patience, honesty, and compassion. He did not ridicule those who struggled to believe but instead sought to understand their concerns, meet them where they were, and walk alongside them as they wrestled with life's biggest questions. This is one of the reasons his writings continue to resonate so powerfully today: they do not assume that faith is easy, but they gently and thoughtfully invite readers into a vision of Christianity that is both intellectually credible and deeply satisfying.

His empathy is especially evident in *The Problem of Pain*, where he does not offer cold, detached philosophical arguments about suffering but instead acknowledges the emotional and existential weight of human pain. He does not minimize the difficulty of trusting in a good God amidst suffering; rather, he carefully walks through the reality of pain, showing that it is both a theological problem and a deeply personal struggle. He invites readers to think critically about suffering while also recognizing the emotional turmoil it creates. His approach models a crucial lesson for discipleship: faith is not about suppressing honest questions but about engaging them with both intellect and compassion.

Later in life, after the death of his wife Joy Davidman, Lewis wrote *A Grief Observed*—a book that stands as one of the most raw and vulnerable reflections on suffering in Christian literature. Unlike *The Problem of Pain*, which offered a reasoned explanation of suffering, *A Grief Observed* is an unfiltered expression of grief, doubt, and anger. In it, Lewis does not try to maintain an image of unwavering faith; instead, he allows himself to ask hard questions, to voice his sorrow, and to wrestle openly with the possibility that his faith might not withstand the weight of his loss. It is this honesty that makes the book so powerful—Lewis does not present discipleship as a journey free from struggle but as one that involves deep wounds, unanswered questions, and moments of profound darkness. And yet, even in his pain, his faith emerges not as a simplistic certainty but as a relationship that is tested, refined, and ultimately deepened.

The Bible affirms this relational and empathetic model of discipleship. The apostle Paul, in 2 Corinthians 1:3-4, describes God as "the Father of mercies and the God of all comfort, who comforts us in all our affliction, so that we may be able to comfort those who are in any affliction, with the comfort with which we ourselves are comforted by God." Discipleship, then, is not merely about imparting theological knowledge but about embodying God's comfort and presence in the lives of others. Just as Lewis's own struggles allowed him to speak with empathy and understanding, believers are called to minister out of their own experiences of God's grace.

Jesus himself modeled this approach in his interactions with those who struggled to believe. In John 20:24-29, he does not scold Thomas for doubting his resurrection but instead invites him to touch his wounds, to see for himself, and to believe. Rather than dismissing doubt as a failure, Jesus meets Thomas where he is, providing the reassurance he needs. Similarly, in Mark 9:24, when a desperate father cries out, "I believe; help my unbelief!" Jesus does not reject him for his wavering faith but responds with compassion and healing. These moments in Scripture reinforce the idea that discipleship should not be rigid and transactional but relational and patient, making space for people to wrestle with faith in the presence of grace.

A church that fosters and practices empathy will be a place where people feel seen, heard, and understood. It will be a place where believers can bring their questions and doubts without fear of condemnation. It will be a place where faith is not presented as a rigid system of beliefs but as a journey that includes struggles, setbacks, and moments of deep joy. This does not mean that truth is compromised or that difficult theological issues are avoided, but it means that discipleship is approached relationally rather than transactionally. It means that believers are given the space to grow at their own pace, to explore their questions without judgment, and to encounter the love of God not as a distant concept but as a lived reality.

Furthermore, we must recognize that the Christian journey of discipleship is not a neat, linear process. It is not something that can be mastered through a series of steps or formulas. Rather, it is a dynamic, lifelong journey—one that involves wrestling with doubt, walking through suffering, and being continually reshaped by the truth of the gospel. If the church is to take discipleship seriously, it must create communities of trust where people can be honest about their struggles. It must cultivate relationships where believers walk together, supporting one another not just with answers but with presence.

In a world where many feel alienated from the church because of past wounds or intellectual doubts, Lewis's example is a reminder that discipleship must begin with empathy. It must seek to understand before it seeks to correct. It must prioritize relationship over argument, presence over instruction, and love over mere knowledge. Paul's exhortation in Galatians 6:2 to "bear one another's burdens, and so fulfill the law of Christ" calls believers to a discipleship model that embraces people in their weakness rather than shaming them for their struggles. When the church embraces this vision, it will not only help believers grow in their faith but will also become a place where the wounded, the skeptical, and the searching can find a home.

This is the kind of discipleship that can transform lives today. By creating a culture of empathy, where people are free to ask hard questions, express their pain, and grow in their faith at their own pace, the church will not only retain believers but will also provide a compelling witness to the world. Jesus declared in John 13:35, "By this all people will know that you are my disciples, if you have love for one another." Love—not debate skills, not moral perfection—is the defining mark of true discipleship.

It is clear then, that Christian discipleship does not happen in isolation. The community of believers plays a crucial role in shaping, encouraging, and sustaining the life of faith. Just as Lewis's own spiritual growth was strengthened through deep friendships and shared theological reflection, he saw the church as essential to the formation of disciples. But what exactly is the church's role in discipleship? Is it merely a gathering of like-minded individuals, or does it serve a deeper purpose?

C. S. Lewis's View of the Church

Lewis's understanding of the church is deeply intertwined with his broader vision of Christian discipleship. He saw the church not as an optional gathering for believers but as the very environment in which discipleship takes place. For Lewis, becoming a Christian was not merely about individual belief or private devotion; it was about being drawn into the life of the body of Christ, where worship and formation go hand in hand. His writings reveal a strong conviction that discipleship cannot flourish in isolation, and that corporate worship is both the means and the goal of Christian growth.

Lewis's journey to appreciating the church was not without struggle. At first, he viewed religious faith as something best cultivated in solitude, through personal reflection and theological study. However, over time, he came to realize that the church was not merely an institution but a divine reality, one that was essential for his own spiritual growth. He admitted in *God in the Dock* that his earlier attempts to live out his faith in isolation had been misguided. He recognized that Christianity is not a faith for individuals alone but for a people—a community bound together by shared worship, sacraments, and life in Christ. He said,

> When I first became a Christian, about fourteen years ago, I thought that I could do it on my own, by retiring to my rooms and reading theology, and I wouldn't go to the churches and Gospel Halls; ... I disliked very much their hymns, which I considered to be fifth-rate poems set to sixth-rate music. But as I went on I saw the great merit of it. I came up against different people of quite different outlooks and different education, and then gradually my conceit just began peeling off. I realized that the hymns (which were just sixth-rate music) were, nevertheless, being sung with devotion and benefit by an old saint in elastic-side boots in the opposite pew, and then you realize that you aren't fit to clean those boots. It gets you out of your solitary conceit.[17]

Lewis's vision of the church was profoundly shaped by his belief that Christianity is not merely a philosophy or a moral system but a transformative reality that shapes people into the likeness of Christ. For Lewis, the church is not simply an institution engaged in various religious activities—preaching, missions, charity, and community gatherings—though these are important. Rather, the fundamental purpose of the church is to "draw men

---

17. Lewis, *God in the Dock*, 61-62.

into Christ, to make them little Christs."[18] This is the heart of the church's mission, and if a church is not fulfilling this purpose, then all of its external works, no matter how impressive, are missing the mark. For this reason, corporate worship and discipleship must walk together.

For Lewis, the church was not an optional addition to the Christian life but the very means by which believers were reoriented toward God. Corporate worship, in this sense, is the primary means through which people are drawn into Christ and shaped by him. In this way, worship is the very heart of discipleship, for it reorders our affections, renews our minds, and deepens our communion with God. In Lewis's own words,

> It is easy to think that the Church has a lot of different objects—education, building, missions, holding services. Just as it is easy to think the State has a lot of different objects—military, political, economic, and what not. But in a way things are much simpler than that. The State exists simply to promote and to protect the ordinary happiness of human beings in this life. A husband and wife chatting over a fire, a couple of friends having a game of darts in a pub, a man reading a book in his own room or digging in his own garden—that is what the State is there for. And unless they are helping to increase and prolong and protect such moments, all the laws, parliaments, armies, courts, police, economics, etc., are simply a waste of time. In the same way the Church exists for nothing else but to draw men into Christ, to make them little Christs. If they are not doing that, all the cathedrals, clergy, missions, sermons, even the Bible itself, are simply a waste of time. God became Man for no other purpose. It is even doubtful, you know, whether the whole universe was created for any other purpose.[19]

Lewis was deeply aware that the church, at its best, was not about maintaining structures, programs, or traditions for their own sake, but about spiritual transformation. The church, he insisted, was about making disciples—about forming believers in the image of Christ. If the church failed in this mission, then all its external activities, no matter how impressive, were in vain. Worship, therefore, was not merely one aspect of church life; it was the lifeblood of Christian formation.

His concerns about worship were not just about theological correctness but about the way worship shapes the soul. In *Letters to Malcolm*, Lewis warned against the constant craving for novelty in worship, arguing

---

18. Lewis, *Mere Christianity*, 171.
19. Lewis, *Mere Christianity*, 171.

that excessive change and experimentation distract from its true purpose.[20] For him, worship was not about personal taste but about being immersed in something greater than oneself, something that lifted the believer beyond individual preference and into the shared life of the church. He emphasized the importance of stability and consistency in worship, believing that true devotion is formed through deep, habitual participation rather than fleeting emotional experiences.

This emphasis on the communal aspect of worship is central to Lewis's understanding of discipleship. In *The Weight of Glory*, he described the church not as a mere collection of individuals but as a living body, where each member is bound to the others through Christ.[21] He warned against the consumerist approach to church, in which believers act as spectators or critics rather than active participants in a spiritual family. In *The Screwtape Letters*, he even has the senior demon advise his apprentice to encourage Christians to hop from church to church, always searching for one that "suits" them best, knowing that such an approach ultimately isolates them from the true purpose of worship.[22] Lewis understood that corporate worship, despite its imperfections, is essential for forming humility, deepening faith, and reminding believers that they are part of something much larger than themselves.

Perhaps one of Lewis's most profound insights into worship comes from *Reflections on the Psalms*, where he wrestles with the idea of heaven as a state of unceasing praise.[23] At first, the notion of eternal worship seemed monotonous to him, but he later realized that true worship is the culmination of joy. He compared it to a moment of rapturous beauty, where delight in something is so overwhelming that the only natural response is to express it. Worship, he came to see, is not simply a duty but the highest fulfillment of the human soul's longing for God. This idea is central to his vision of discipleship—believers are not merely being trained to obey moral laws or to think correctly about God; they are being drawn into an ever-deepening relationship with him, one that will ultimately find its consummation in worship. In Lewis's own words, "The Scotch catechism says that man's chief end is 'to glorify God and enjoy him forever'. But we shall then know that

---

20. Lewis, *Letters to Malcolm: Chiefly on Prayer*, 13.
21. Lewis, *Weight of Glory*, 166.
22. Lewis, *The Screwtape Letters*, 12-13.
23. Lewis, *Reflections on the Psalms*, 93-97.

these are the same thing. Fully to enjoy is to glorify. In commanding us to glorify him, God is inviting us to enjoy him."[24]

Lewis's vision of the church is profoundly relevant in a time when many view faith as a private matter, separate from communal worship. The modern tendency to emphasize personal spirituality apart from the church is, from his perspective, a dangerous distortion. He reminds us that the church is not merely a human organization; it is a divine institution, established by Christ and sustained by His presence.

It is in corporate worship that believers are reminded of this reality, that they are not alone in their faith, and that their individual discipleship is part of something far greater. If the church exists to make disciples, and discipleship finds its highest expression in worship, then it follows that any vision of the church that neglects the worship of the church is incomplete. Worship fuels discipleship, for it continually reorients the heart toward God, renews the mind in His truth, and binds the community of believers together in shared devotion. In this way, Lewis's vision of the church calls modern Christians back to a fuller, richer understanding of their faith—one in which discipleship and worship are inseparable.

Winning People, Not Arguments

Lewis's apologetic method was never about winning arguments—it was about winning people. He understood that faith is not just an abstract system of beliefs to be affirmed but a way of seeing reality, a call to transformation, and an invitation into a greater story. His defense of Christianity appealed to the whole person—engaging the mind with reason, awakening the heart through imagination, and nurturing spiritual growth within community.

This threefold approach remains vital for discipleship today. In a world where skepticism abounds, intellectual engagement is necessary to provide compelling reasons for belief. Yet reason alone is not enough—people must also feel the weight of truth, experience the beauty of the gospel, and be drawn into the narrative of redemption. And most importantly, faith is not meant to be lived in isolation. Authentic Christian discipleship happens in community, where questions can be asked, struggles shared, and spiritual growth fostered through genuine relationships.

---

24. Lewis, *Reflections on the Psalms*, 97.

In the next chapter, we will turn our attention to the realities of our post-Christian age. How do we disciple believers in a world that no longer assumes Christianity as its foundation? What does faithfulness look like when the culture is no longer merely indifferent but actively resistant to Christian claims? Building on Lewis's insights, we will explore a discipleship model that speaks to the unique challenges of our time, equipping believers not just to defend their faith, but to embody it in a way that transforms lives and communities.

Chapter 5

A Discipleship Model for the Post-Christian World

IN AN AGE WHERE skepticism toward religious belief is widespread, institutional faith is met with indifference, and entertainment-driven distractions shape cultural priorities, the church must recover a holistic model of discipleship—one that engages both the mind and heart while restoring the richness of Christian community. Faith cannot be sustained by intellectual instruction alone, nor can it thrive merely on fleeting emotional experiences. In a post-Christian society dominated by secular ideologies—where biblical literacy is waning and people are catechized more by algorithms than by Scripture—discipleship must go deeper.

The challenge before the church is not merely to transmit information, but to cultivate resilient, thoughtful, and relationally engaged followers of Christ—believers who can navigate doubt, recognize beauty, and embody the gospel in a world often apathetic or even hostile to faith.

As we've seen with a little help from Lewis, an effective model of discipleship rests on three foundational elements: reason, imagination, and community. Yet each of these dimensions faces serious cultural headwinds that hinder spiritual formation. In this chapter, we will explore three particularly pressing challenges to discipleship in our cultural moment—challenges that serve as clear and relevant examples of broader patterns. They are not the only threats to Christian formation today, but they are among the most visible and influential.

First, we will examine how confusion surrounding gender and sexuality reflects a deeper crisis of identity and self-understanding, and how the church can speak biblical truth into that confusion by grounding identity in God's design rather than self-construction. Second, we will consider how entertainment and digital distractions have numbed our capacity for reflection and wonder, and how a renewed emphasis on beauty and meaning can help reawaken the soul. Finally, we will address the pervasive individualism that isolates believers and erodes deep belonging, calling the church to reclaim its role as a formative, relational community.

Taken together, these challenges illuminate the need for a discipleship model that forms both intellect and affections in the context of meaningful relationships. With the help of C. S. Lewis, we are reminded that discipleship in a post-Christian world must be rational enough to offer truth in a confused age, imaginative enough to awaken wonder, and communal enough to create spaces of belonging in a fragmented culture. Only a discipleship that speaks to the whole person—heart and mind—can shape believers who are both faithful and fruitful in a world desperate for grace and truth.

The Challenge of Identity and Sexuality

If discipleship is to be effective in a post-Christian world, it must address the real struggles and questions people face today. Cultural shifts surrounding identity and sexuality have created one of the most difficult and divisive challenges for the church. Many people, both inside and outside the faith, wrestle with how to reconcile biblical teachings with contemporary views on identity, inclusion, and personal freedom. For discipleship to be meaningful, it must provide more than simple moral answers or rigid prohibitions. It must engage deeply, offering both truth and compassion, conviction and grace. How can the church disciple believers in a world where identity is increasingly self-defined? How can we speak about biblical sexuality in a way that is both faithful and compelling?

In our post-Christian age, identity has become one of the most contested and deeply personal issues in human life. The modern world increasingly views identity as a fluid and self-constructed reality, where individuals define themselves based on internal desires, emotions, and perceptions rather than external truths. Nowhere is this shift more evident than in the conversation surrounding gender and sexuality. What was once understood as biological and given—male and female—has, in much of Western culture, been redefined as a matter of personal identification and self-expression.[1]

At the heart of these cultural changes is the rise of expressive individualism, a concept described by philosopher Charles Taylor in *A Secular Age* (2007). Expressive individualism asserts that the highest good is for individuals to discover and express their authentic inner selves, free from external constraints, whether they be religious, social, or biological. This worldview holds that personal identity is constructed, not received, and that true fulfillment comes through the uninhibited expression of one's desires. The modern world has shifted toward a more subjective understanding of identity. In the philosophy of existentialism and postmodernism, for example, meaning is no longer found in something transcendent; rather, it is constructed from within the individual. As Taylor argues, we have moved from an "enchanted" world, filled with meaning given by God, to a "disenchanted" one, where the individual is left to create a personal sense of purpose.

Philosopher Alasdair MacIntyre, in *After Virtue* (2007), argues that contemporary ethics have been reduced to emotivism—where moral claims are based solely on personal feelings rather than any transcendent standard. In this framework, gender and sexuality are not fixed realities but flexible constructs, subject to personal preference and cultural redefinition. This shift makes it difficult for many to accept biblical teaching on gender and sexuality, as it is perceived as restrictive or even oppressive. However, the biblical vision is not about limiting personal freedom but about aligning human life with God's good design, which leads to true flourishing.

Christian philosopher Nancy Pearcey, in *Love Thy Body* (2018), critiques the dualistic thinking that separates the body from the self, treating biological sex as irrelevant to personal identity. She argues that this perspective devalues the body and ultimately undermines human dignity. Pearcey explains that the biblical worldview affirms the unity of body and soul, recognizing that the body is not an obstacle to personal identity but an essential part of God's design. This insight is crucial for discipleship, as it provides a framework to help believers understand and embrace their embodied existence rather than seeing their bodies as problems to be overcome.

---

1. For a detailed account of the crisis of the modern culture, I recommend Carl Trueman, *The Rise and Triumph of the Modern Self* (2020).

Furthermore, secular narratives increasingly define human dignity in terms of sexual identity. Modern culture has moved beyond seeing sexuality as an important aspect of human life to treating it as central to one's identity. Many are taught that discovering and affirming their sexual orientation or gender identity is essential to finding meaning and purpose. This is why traditional Christian teachings on gender and sexuality are often perceived as not merely outdated but harmful—because they challenge the notion that self-expression is the key to human flourishing.

These cultural shifts have led to several practical problems that affect individuals, families, and communities in profound ways. One major consequence is the growing confusion and anxiety surrounding identity formation, especially among young people. In a world where identity is seen as self-generated and endlessly customizable, many are burdened with the pressure to "find themselves" without any objective reference points. This has contributed to a rise in mental health struggles, including anxiety, depression, and a sense of alienation. When meaning is constructed solely from within, the self becomes both the question and the answer—an unsustainable weight that the human soul was never meant to carry alone.

Another practical issue is the breakdown of shared moral frameworks and the resulting fragmentation of social life. When identity is defined by personal feeling rather than by shared truths, it becomes increasingly difficult to maintain cohesive communities. Public discourse becomes charged with emotion rather than reason, and disagreement is often seen not as a matter of intellectual or moral difference but as a personal attack. In such a climate, biblical teachings are not just rejected—they are vilified as oppressive. This leaves the church with the challenge of speaking truth in love to a culture that interprets moral clarity as intolerance. As expressive individualism becomes more entrenched, the church must both understand these underlying worldviews and respond with compassion, clarity, and courage—offering not just answers, but a better story of what it means to be human.

Furthermore, the devaluation of the body and the detachment of identity from biological reality have led to confusion in legal, educational, and medical systems. Institutions that once operated on the assumption of stable categories—such as male and female—now struggle to navigate ever-shifting definitions. Children are being introduced to complex issues of gender identity at increasingly young ages, often without the guidance of parents or clear moral frameworks. Medical interventions, such as puberty blockers and gender reassignment surgeries, are promoted as acts of liberation, yet often come with long-term consequences that are not fully understood. In this context, the church must reassert the goodness of the created order and the dignity of the body, offering discipleship that not only forms the mind but also restores a biblical view of embodied identity.

The biblical vision of identity, sexuality, and gender offers a radically different foundation, one that is both rooted in truth and filled with grace. If discipleship is to be effective in a post-Christian world, it must address these issues in a way that is both biblically faithful and pastorally wise. The church cannot afford to remain silent or retreat in fear, nor can it simply rely on rigid prohibitions without offering a compelling, life-giving alternative. Instead, the church must recover and teach a rich, biblical anthropology—one that restores the beauty and dignity of human identity as designed by God.

What, then, is the solution to this identity crisis of our modern culture? For Lewis, the answer lies in the gospel of Jesus Christ. The self, fractured by sin and burdened by the weight of autonomy, can be redeemed only through union with Christ. This redemption involves both a death and a resurrection: we must die to our old, sinful selves to be raised to new life in Christ.

Lewis speaks of the eternal destiny that awaits those who are united to Christ. He writes, "The load, or weight, or burden of my neighbor's glory should be laid daily on my back, a load so heavy that only humility can carry it, and the backs of the proud will be broken."[2] Here, Lewis emphasizes that our identity is bound up not only in our relationship with God but also in our relationships with others. To be truly human is to reflect the love of God to our neighbors, bearing the weight of their glory as we walk in humility and love.

The foundation of biblical identity is not self-creation but divine design. Scripture begins with the affirmation that human beings are made in the image of God: "So God created man in His own image, in the image of God He created him; male and female He created them." (Genesis 1:27). This passage establishes two crucial truths. First, human worth and dignity do not come from self-definition or societal validation but from the fact that we are created by God in his image. Every person—regardless of gender, sexual orientation, or personal struggles—is inherently valuable because they reflect the image of the Creator. Second, gender

---

2. Lewis, *The Weight of Glory*, 45.

is not an arbitrary social construct but a divine distinction, woven into creation by God's intentional design. Scripture presents male and female as complementary, equal in dignity yet distinct in purpose, designed to reflect God's wisdom and order.

The prevailing secular belief that human beings can redefine their own bodies and identities as they see fit is ultimately rooted in a rejection of God's authority over creation. Yet, despite the cultural insistence that true freedom comes from rejecting external constraints, Scripture teaches that real freedom is found in living according to God's design. Jesus reaffirms the goodness of this design when he teaches on marriage and sexuality, pointing back to Genesis: "Have you not read that He who created them from the beginning made them male and female, and said, 'Therefore a man shall leave his father and his mother and hold fast to his wife, and the two shall become one flesh'?" (Matt 19:4–5)

Far from being a cultural construct that can be redefined at will, gender is a sacred part of human identity, reflecting the divine order and purpose established at creation. Likewise, human sexuality is presented in Scripture as a gift from God, designed for the covenantal union of marriage between one man and one woman (Gen 2:24). In contrast to the contemporary claim that personal fulfillment is found in unrestricted sexual expression, the biblical vision calls for sexual holiness, recognizing that our bodies are not our own but belong to God (1 Cor 6:19–20).

While secular culture claims that fulfillment comes through self-creation, the gospel proclaims that true freedom is found in surrendering to God's design. Jesus' call to deny oneself and follow him (Luke 9:23) is not a burden but an invitation to embrace an identity rooted in God's love rather than in the shifting sands of personal desire. The church must, therefore, disciple believers to understand that their worth is not determined by sexual identity but by being adopted as sons and daughters of God (Rom 8:15–17).

The crisis of the modern culture is, at its core, a spiritual crisis. It is a symptom of humanity's attempt to live without God. But as Lewis reminds us, true freedom, fulfillment, and identity are found not in self-assertion but in self-surrender to Christ. As Jesus said, "Whoever wants to save their life will lose it, but whoever loses their life for me will save it" (Luke 9:24). In Christ, we discover that losing ourselves is the only way to find our true selves.

A DISCIPLESHIP MODEL FOR THE POST-CHRISTIAN WORLD

In an age of confusion, the church has the opportunity to offer clarity—not by conforming to cultural trends but by presenting a compelling, biblically grounded vision of what it means to be human. True discipleship does not simply react to the cultural moment; it offers a better story. And in Christ, that story is one of redemption, transformation, and the restoration of identity to its rightful place: in the hands of our Creator.

The Challenge of Digital Distractions

Another threat to Christian discipleship in the post-Christian world is not outright persecution, nor is it intellectual skepticism alone—it is the sheer difficulty of maintaining attention in an age of relentless digital distractions. As smartphones, social media, and algorithm-driven entertainment dominate daily life, our ability to think deeply, reflect prayerfully, and engage meaningfully with God's word is steadily eroding. The very habits that have historically formed strong disciples—contemplative prayer, deep meditation on Scripture, and rich, communal worship—are now being overshadowed by the endless stream of notifications, digital amusements, and fleeting entertainment.

For many, discipleship today competes with the omnipresence of digital distractions. Even believers with the best intentions often find themselves scrolling through social media rather than spending time in God's presence, consuming hours of online entertainment rather than meditating on eternal truths. In a world where people are pulled in a thousand different directions, how can discipleship survive? How can the church cultivate focus, silence, and depth in an age where people struggle to sit still and be present before God?

Modern Western culture is not merely shaped by technology—it is driven by an economy that profits from keeping people entertained, distracted, and perpetually consuming. The rise of social media, streaming services, and digital platforms has created an environment where attention is monetized. The more time users spend scrolling, watching, and clicking, the more profitable they become for advertisers and tech companies.

Neil Postman's *Amusing Ourselves to Death* (1985) presents a sobering critique of how modern media, particularly television and mass entertainment, has reshaped the way people process information and engage with reality. He contrasts the dystopian warnings of George Orwell (*1984*) and Aldous Huxley (*Brave New World*), arguing that the real threat to society is not totalitarian oppression but passive distraction. In an entertainment-driven culture, important discussions about truth, virtue, and meaning are drowned out by a constant stream of amusement. Rather than being forcefully silenced, people willingly disengage from serious thought, prioritizing spectacle over substance. Postman warns that when public discourse is reduced to soundbites, images, and sensationalism, the result is not an informed citizenry but a distracted one—one that no longer values deep thinking, moral reflection, or truth itself. This insight is even more relevant today, as social media algorithms carefully curate content designed to keep users engaged—offering just enough stimulation to maintain interest but never enough depth to require serious thought.

Nicholas Carr, in *The Shallows* (2010), describes how constant digital stimulation is physically rewiring human brains, making deep thinking and sustained reflection increasingly difficult. The digital age is shaping people to prefer quick bursts of information over long-form engagement, encouraging surface-level consumption rather than deep contemplation. For Christian discipleship, this shift presents a profound challenge. If growing in faith requires sustained engagement with Scripture, prayer, and theological reflection, but the modern mind is being trained for short attention spans and shallow consumption, how can believers be shaped into the image of Christ?

The danger of this cultural shift is not just intellectual shallowness, but spiritual numbness. Blaise Pascal, in *Pensées*, observed that human beings seek distraction to avoid facing the deeper realities of existence—our mortality, our need for God, and the state of our souls. He wrote, "All of humanity's problems stem from man's inability to sit quietly in a room alone."[3] In other words, the pursuit of constant stimulation is often an attempt to escape the weight of ultimate questions.

Many digital distractions function as a form of escapism. Entertainment, social media, and endless scrolling allow people to avoid dealing with personal struggles, existential questions, and, ultimately, the voice of God. When entertainment and constant stimulation become a refuge, silence and solitude become unbearable. This is a significant problem for discipleship, as spiritual growth requires periods of stillness before God, attentive listening, and the willingness to engage with the depths of the soul.

Lewis offers profound insights into the challenge of digital distraction, even though he wrote long before the advent of social media and

---

3. Pascal, *Pensées*, 37.

smartphones. His warnings about the dangers of shallow thinking, constant noise, and passive entertainment are remarkably prescient in the modern world. In *The Screwtape Letters*, Lewis portrays the demonic strategy of keeping humans spiritually disengaged not through overt argumentation but through endless distraction:

> You will find that anything or nothing is sufficient to attract his wandering attention. You no longer need a good book, which he really likes, to keep him from his prayers or his work or his sleep; a column of advertisements in yesterday's paper will do. You can make him waste his time not only in conversation he enjoys with people whom he likes but in conversations with those he cares nothing about on subjects that bore him.[4]

Lewis understood that distraction is not neutral—it is a tool that keeps people from engaging with truth, from reflecting deeply, and ultimately, from encountering God.

If discipleship is about becoming more like Christ, then it requires intentional engagement with him. To counteract the numbing effects of entertainment and digital distraction, the church must reclaim the role of imagination in discipleship. The human heart longs for beauty, transcendence, and wonder—things that modern entertainment often promises but fails to deliver. Instead of merely warning against the dangers of entertainment, the church must present the gospel as the ultimate source of beauty and meaning. This means recovering a vision of the Christian faith that is not just intellectually true but imaginatively compelling.

The Bible itself is filled with imaginative storytelling, poetic imagery, and symbolic richness designed to capture the heart as well as the mind. The Psalms use vivid metaphors to describe God's majesty, the prophets speak in striking visions, and Jesus teaches through parables that engage the imagination. Scripture does not merely present dry theological propositions—it paints a picture of reality that is meant to be seen, felt, and experienced. Christian discipleship must reclaim this holistic approach, inviting people not only to understand the faith but to be captivated by it. If discipleship is to flourish in the digital age, believers must actively reclaim their time, attention, and spiritual focus. This will not happen accidentally; it requires intentional practices that create space for God amidst the noise. The church's task is to reawaken this sense of wonder,

---

4. Lewis, *The Screwtape Letters* (1942), letter 12.

helping people see the beauty of creation, the depth of God's love, and the grandeur of redemption.

First, believers must cultivate habits of silence and solitude. In an age where constant connectivity is the norm, setting aside time to be alone with God is a radical act of faith. Jesus himself regularly withdrew to quiet places to pray, demonstrating that deep communion with the Father requires undistracted presence. Modern Christians must recover this discipline, establishing daily rhythms of stillness before God, free from the pull of notifications and entertainment.

Second, churches must create countercultural spaces where believers can slow down and engage deeply. This means fostering environments where long-form Scripture meditation, theological reflection, and rich community discussions are prioritized over hurried consumption of religious content. The goal is not just to provide information but to shape affections and desires toward what is truly good, beautiful, and lasting.

Third, discipleship must include teaching believers how to steward their digital habits wisely. This does not mean rejecting technology altogether, but rather learning how to use it without being mastered by it. This might involve setting limits on social media, practicing digital Sabbaths, or intentionally curating content that enriches rather than distracts. The goal is to create a life where digital engagement serves spiritual formation rather than undermining it.

Ultimately, the challenge of digital distraction is not just about time management or focus—it is about desire. If the heart is captivated by trivial entertainment, it will have little room for the things of God. But if the heart is stirred by the beauty of the gospel, digital distractions will lose their hold. For this reason, Christian discipleship must awaken people from spiritual lethargy, reorient their desires, and cultivate a love for what is true, good, and beautiful. The solution is not merely to resist distraction but to replace it with something far greater—a life of deep, joyful communion with God. Only when believers see that their deepest longings will never be satisfied by entertainment, consumer goods, or fleeting digital amusements will they turn to the One who alone can satisfy the soul.

The Challenge of Individualism

While digital distractions fragment our attention, individualism isolates our souls. The modern world champions self-sufficiency, personal expression, and autonomy as the highest ideals. Faith, however, calls us into something countercultural—a life of dependence on God and interdependence with others. For many, the idea of submitting to a community, to spiritual authority, or even to God's will is difficult, if not offensive. The church must disciple believers in a way that challenges the idol of self-sufficiency while demonstrating the beauty of life together in Christ. How can discipleship flourish in a culture that views faith as a private, individual journey rather than a shared and communal calling?

This individualistic mindset shapes how people view relationships, identity, and even faith. The idea that one can be "spiritual but not religious," or that faith is a private matter disconnected from communal life, has led to a widespread erosion of deep, committed relationships within the church. The crisis of individualism is not just a sociological concern—it is a spiritual crisis that directly affects Christian discipleship. Without meaningful Christian community, faith becomes shallow, fragmented, and vulnerable to cultural drift.

Sociologist Robert Putnam, in *Bowling Alone* (2000), describes how traditional social institutions—churches, civic groups, and local communities—have experienced a sharp decline in participation. He argues that fewer people engage in deep, long-term communal relationships, opting instead for transient and loosely connected social networks. This trend has only accelerated with the rise of digital technology, where online interactions often replace face-to-face relationships. While social media provides unprecedented connectivity, it paradoxically fosters isolation, as people substitute curated digital interactions for real, embodied community.

The effects of radical individualism on discipleship are profound. Many Christians today approach church with a consumer mentality, evaluating it based on personal preferences rather than as a covenant community where they are called to belong and serve. The rise of "church hopping" and "virtual church" culture reflects a broader trend where faith is privatized and participation is conditional. Dietrich Bonhoeffer emphasized that Christian faith cannot exist apart from authentic community. He wrote, "The Christian needs another Christian who speaks God's word to him. He needs him again and again when he becomes uncertain and discouraged, for by himself he cannot help himself."[5] For Bonhoeffer, discipleship is not merely about individual belief but about being shaped through the daily reality of shared

---

5. Bonhoeffer, *Life Together*, 23.

life with fellow believers. The church must recover this vision if it hopes to nurture disciples in an age of relational disintegration.

Lewis understood that faith must be lived out in the context of the church, where believers are both encouraged and challenged. He further critiques the modern tendency to treat church as a matter of personal preference, warning in *The Screwtape Letters* that a consumerist approach to worship turns the church into a mere social club rather than a transformative body of believers. He saw worship as a training ground for humility, where one's personal tastes and individualism are set aside in favor of something greater—participation in the body of Christ. For Lewis, Christian community was not optional; it was an essential means of grace through which believers grow in faith, resist self-centeredness, and learn to love one another as Christ commanded. His perspective calls modern Christians to reject the isolation of individualism and embrace the beauty and necessity of shared spiritual life in the church.

From the beginning, God designed human beings for relationship, declaring in Genesis 2:18, "It is not good that the man should be alone." This principle extends beyond marriage to the broader reality of human interdependence. The Old Testament is filled with examples of covenant community, where Israel's identity was shaped not merely by individual belief but by collective worship, shared traditions, and communal responsibility. In the New Testament, Jesus did not call isolated followers but gathered a group of disciples who lived, learned, and ministered together. The early church, as described in Acts 2:42–47, was characterized by shared meals, mutual support, and communal worship—a radical contrast to the hyper-individualistic culture of today.

Paul's epistles reinforce the necessity of Christian community, using metaphors such as the "body of Christ" to illustrate the interconnectedness of believers. In 1 Corinthians 12:12–27, he emphasizes that no member of the body can function independently, stating, "The eye cannot say to the hand, 'I have no need of you.'" This challenges the modern assumption that faith is a purely personal matter. The biblical vision of the church is not a collection of isolated individuals pursuing God separately, but a family bound together in covenantal love, sacrificial service, and shared mission.

Jean Vanier, founder of the *L'Arche* communities, spent his life cultivating spiritual communities that welcomed the marginalized and emphasized the necessity of belonging. In *Community and Growth*, he wrote, "To love someone is to reveal to them their beauty and value, to say to them through our attitude: 'You are beautiful. You are important. I trust you. You can trust yourself.'"[6] His work demonstrated that authentic Christian community is not merely about shared belief but about living out love in tangible, sacrificial ways. True belonging happens not when people find a church that meets their needs, but when they commit themselves to a church where they are needed.

The erosion of community in modern society has had devastating effects on mental and spiritual health. Loneliness and social isolation have been linked to increased anxiety, depression, and even physical illness. A study by the Harvard T. H. Chan School of Public Health found that social isolation is as detrimental to health as smoking 15 cigarettes a day.[7] If secular researchers recognize the necessity of belonging for human flourishing, how much more should the church emphasize the spiritual and relational necessity of deep community?

To counteract the crisis of individualism, the church must reclaim its role as a true spiritual family. This requires moving beyond a consumer-driven model of faith, where participation is measured by attendance and content consumption, to a relational model, where believers are actively engaged in one another's lives.

Eugene Peterson critiques the modern church's tendency to adopt a consumer-driven model, focusing on marketing strategies and numerical growth rather than fostering genuine spiritual communities. He emphasizes that true discipleship is not the product of programs or strategic plans but emerges from long-term, faithful relationships where believers accompany one another through life's challenges and spiritual development. Peterson underscores that the essence of pastoral work involves "paying attention and calling attention to 'what is going on right now' between men and women, with each other and with God."[8]

Practically, shared experiences—prayer, confession, communal worship, and service—create the bonds necessary for true spiritual formation. True belonging is not found in seeking a perfect community that caters to personal desires, but in committing to an imperfect community where love, forgiveness, and sacrifice shape people into the likeness of Christ. In other words, the challenge of individualism cannot be solved through superficial programs or casual social gatherings. It requires a reorientation of how

---

6. Vanier, *Community and Growth*, 16.
7. Holt-Lunstad et al., "Advancing Social Connection," 517-30.
8. Peterson, *The Pastor*, 5-7.

believers view the church—not as an optional addition to their personal faith, but as the very context in which faith is lived and sustained.

The Path to *Moralistic Therapeutic Deism*: A Crisis in Discipleship

The cultural challenges of identity confusion, digital distraction, and radical individualism are not merely external forces shaping the secular world; they have deeply influenced how people understand and practice faith within the church. When identity is self-constructed rather than received from God, when constant entertainment replaces deep reflection, and when faith is reduced to a private journey rather than a communal calling, Christianity becomes increasingly therapeutic, moralistic, and disconnected from biblical truth. These cultural currents have not simply remained outside the church—they have subtly reshaped the expectations and priorities of many believers, contributing to what sociologists have termed *Moralistic Therapeutic Deism* (MTD), a faith that prioritizes personal happiness, vague moralism, and a distant, non-intervening God over the transformative call of the gospel.[9]

This modern religious outlook, while borrowing Christian language, offers a God who affirms rather than transforms, comforts rather than convicts, and exists primarily to help people feel good rather than to call them into holiness and mission. In other words, this is not merely an alternative belief system; it is the natural outcome of a cultural landscape shaped by the very challenges facing the church today: the identity crisis surrounding gender and sexuality, the numbing effects of digital distraction, and the erosion of deep, committed Christian community. These forces have reshaped how people understand themselves, engage with reality, and relate to others, leading to a shallow, individualistic spirituality that values personal happiness over discipleship, therapeutic affirmation over transformation, and moralistic self-improvement over the grace of the gospel.

MTD describes a worldview in which God functions primarily as a distant figure who encourages moral behavior, provides therapeutic comfort, and remains largely uninvolved in human affairs unless summoned in

---

9. For further discussion on MTD and its impact on the church, see Dean, *Almost Christian: What the Faith of Our Teenagers Is Telling the American Church* (2010); Noble, *Disruptive Witness* (2018); Carter, "What Is Moralistic Therapeutic Deism?" *The Gospel Coalition* (April 18, 2018).

times of need. The term was coined in 2005 following a study on American teenagers' religious beliefs, which revealed that many embraced a spirituality largely detached from historic Christian doctrine. However, subsequent research has shown that MTD is not merely a teenage phenomenon but reflects a broader cultural shift, shaping the way many Americans—including adults—understand and practice faith.[10]

First, in a world where personal identity is no longer seen as something received from God but constructed by the self, faith becomes another tool for self-definition rather than a call to surrender and transformation. The widespread influence of expressive individualism reinforces the idea that the highest good is the freedom to be whatever one desires. In this framework, God becomes little more than an approving figure who exists to affirm rather than challenge, support rather than correct. The church's reluctance to address these identity questions with biblical clarity has left many Christians embracing a faith that seeks validation over repentance, self-fulfillment over obedience. Without a theological foundation for human identity, many have adopted an MTD perspective where faith serves as an accessory to self-realization rather than a call to take up the cross and follow Christ.

Second, another major factor fueling MTD is the culture of digital distraction. The omnipresence of entertainment and social media has reshaped how people process truth, making deep contemplation, serious theological reflection, and sustained discipleship increasingly rare. Today's digital habits reinforce an instinctive preference for instant gratification over slow, disciplined growth—an attitude that easily transfers into matters of faith. If people struggle to focus on anything beyond momentary pleasure, how can they be expected to persevere in a discipleship process that demands patience, suffering, and long-term transformation? The church, too often mirroring the culture, has sometimes adopted a "seeker-sensitive" model that prioritizes entertainment and emotional experience over substantive teaching and spiritual formation. The result is a form of Christianity that fits neatly into the therapeutic ethos of MTD—where God is expected to provide immediate relief but not to shape character through discipline and endurance.

---

10. This new research was published by the Cultural Research Center at Arizona Christian University, *AWVI 2021: Release #02: Introducing America's Most Popular Worldview—Moralistic Therapeutic Deism* (2021).

Finally, the decline of committed Christian community has further entrenched MTD within the church. Faith has become increasingly privatized, reduced to personal spiritual experience rather than a communal journey. The modern emphasis on autonomy and self-sufficiency has led many to view the church as optional or transactional rather than as an essential context for spiritual growth. When church involvement is seen as a matter of convenience rather than covenantal commitment, faith becomes more about self-improvement and emotional uplift—hallmarks of MTD—rather than about sanctification through shared life in the body of Christ. Without the accountability and depth of true Christian community, faith naturally drifts toward a therapeutic model that seeks comfort rather than challenge, affirmation rather than correction.

We see these dynamics play out in practical ways within the life of the church. For instance, many churches feel increasing pressure to structure worship services around entertainment value rather than theological depth. Sermons are shortened and simplified, music is designed to elicit emotional highs, and silence or liturgical practices that require contemplation are minimized or eliminated altogether. While the intention may be to make church more accessible or engaging, the unintended effect is often a congregation that is less equipped to engage Scripture deeply, less patient with spiritual formation, and more oriented toward personal preference than communal transformation. This feeds into the MTD framework, where the primary goal of worship becomes feeling good rather than encountering the holy, sovereign God who calls His people to repentance, obedience, and awe.

Another manifestation of these challenges is the rise of "DIY discipleship," where individuals pick and choose spiritual content online—podcasts, Instagram devotionals, YouTube sermons—without accountability, pastoral guidance, or participation in the life of a local body. While digital resources can be beneficial supplements, they often replace meaningful church engagement and can foster a consumer mindset toward spiritual growth. Many believers attend church sporadically or view Christian community as optional, engaging only when convenient or when a particular program meets their felt needs. This weakens the bonds of fellowship, discipleship, and service that are essential to a biblical vision of the church. The result is a shallow spirituality where growth is stunted because it is no longer rooted in the rhythms of worship, the sacraments, mutual encouragement, and the bearing of one another's burdens—all of which are indispensable for true transformation into the likeness of Christ.

If the church is to resist the shallow, self-focused spirituality of *Moralistic Therapeutic Deism* (MTD), it must reclaim a holistic model of discipleship that engages both the mind and the heart. As we propose in this book, Lewis's threefold approach—reason, imagination, and community—offers a compelling way forward in forming disciples who can withstand the pressures of secular culture while growing in a faith that is intellectually rich, spiritually vibrant, and deeply rooted in the life of the church.

Reason challenges the thin theological assumptions of MTD, grounding believers in a faith that is intellectually robust and deeply rooted in truth. Lewis insisted that Christianity is rational and must be defended as such, calling believers to engage deeply with Scripture, theology, and the great tradition of Christian thought rather than settling for a feel-good spirituality devoid of substance. The church must not only teach doctrine but equip believers to think critically and discern cultural narratives, resisting the impulse to prioritize emotional experience over doctrinal depth. A faith that cannot stand up to scrutiny will inevitably collapse under pressure, but one that is shaped by rigorous intellectual engagement will endure.

Imagination provides a way of countering the numbing effects of entertainment culture. Rather than attempting to compete with digital distractions by making worship and teaching more entertaining, the church must reclaim the beauty and wonder of the Christian story. Lewis understood that people are shaped not only by logical arguments but by compelling narratives that stir the soul. The gospel is not merely a set of abstract truths; it is the greatest story ever told, and the church must present it as such—through rich storytelling, vibrant worship, and a renewed sense of wonder that awakens spiritual hunger. In an age of cynicism and superficiality, the church must help believers recover a sense of awe at the grandeur of God and his redemptive work.

Community is the essential pillar of discipleship, providing the relational foundation that sustains faith. The antidote to radical individualism is a church that functions as the family of God, where believers find belonging, accountability, and spiritual formation. Lewis emphasized that faith is not a solitary endeavor but one lived out in the fellowship of other believers. A privatized, consumer-driven approach to Christianity—where faith is treated as an individual preference rather than a shared calling—undermines the very nature of discipleship. The church must reclaim the biblical vision of covenantal relationships, fostering deep, lasting commitments to one another in Christ. This means prioritizing meaningful relationships over religious programs, practicing hospitality, and ensuring that discipleship is not reduced to a classroom experience but is woven into the rhythms of everyday life.

MTD is a symptom of a deeper crisis in modern discipleship. It is the product of a culture that has lost its theological foundation, become addicted to distraction, and abandoned the communal nature of faith. If the church is to counter the shallow individualism of our post-Christian society, it must reclaim the formative power of embodied, relational faith. As we have seen, discipleship is not merely about imparting knowledge or moral instruction—it is about creating a space where people can encounter the reality of Christ through shared life and authentic community. At its core, Christian formation is deeply relational, and one of the most tangible ways this is expressed is through hospitality. In a fragmented world where isolation and consumer-driven faith have become the norm, the practice of hospitality stands as a radical, countercultural witness. It is within the context of meals shared, burdens carried, and lives intertwined that faith is deepened, wounds are healed, and true discipleship takes root. If the church hopes to form resilient disciples, it must begin by recovering the biblical call to hospitality.

Hospitality as a Foundation for Discipleship

Throughout Scripture, the home is a place of ministry, teaching, and spiritual formation. The early church did not primarily grow through large events or formal institutions but through the ordinary rhythms of life shared around tables, in homes, and within small communities. Hospitality creates space for relationships to flourish, for the faith to be modeled in daily life, and for discipleship to become deeply personal rather than merely programmatic.

In both the Old and New Testaments, hospitality is a hallmark of God's people. Abraham welcomed strangers and was blessed by divine visitation (Gen 18:1–8). The Israelites were commanded to love the sojourner, remembering that they too were once strangers in a foreign land (Deut 10:19). In the New Testament, Jesus frequently ministered in the context of meals, using table fellowship as a means of teaching, healing, and revealing the kingdom of God. He dined with tax collectors and sinners (Luke 5:29–32), ate with his disciples in moments of deep instruction (John 13), and ultimately gave his body and blood in the context of a meal (Luke 22:14–20). Hospitality was not an incidental part of his ministry; it was central to how he formed his followers.

The early church continued this practice. The book of Acts presents a model of discipleship in which believers "broke bread in their homes and ate together with glad and sincere hearts" (Acts 2:46). Paul, writing to the Romans, exhorted them to "contribute to the needs of the saints and seek to show hospitality" (Rom 12:13). Peter similarly instructed believers to "show hospitality to one another without grumbling" (1 Pet 4:9). The practice of welcoming others into one's home was not seen as an extra act of kindness but as an integral part of what it meant to be the church.

Hospitality in discipleship is vital because it transforms Christian relationships from formal acquaintances to deep, life-giving friendships. When believers gather in homes for meals, prayer, and conversation, they move beyond a surface-level faith and enter into a relational discipleship where struggles, joys, and questions can be shared honestly. A church that prioritizes community and hospitality creates an environment where people are not only known but also loved, encouraged, and challenged to grow in Christ.

Lewis's commitment to hospitality significantly influenced his approach to discipleship and community building. At his home, *The Kilns*, Lewis created a welcoming environment where friends, students, and colleagues could engage in meaningful conversations about faith, literature, and life. This practice of opening his home fostered deep relationships and facilitated personal spiritual growth among his guests.[11]

Additionally, Lewis was an active member of the *Inklings*, an informal literary group that met regularly to discuss their works-in-progress. These gatherings, often held in Lewis's rooms at Magdalen College or local Oxford pubs like *The Eagle and Child*, exemplified a form of communal hospitality that encouraged mutual support and intellectual stimulation among members. Through these practices, Lewis demonstrated that hospitality—whether through opening one's home or fostering supportive communities—is foundational to effective discipleship and the nurturing of faith.[12]

---

11. Read more about Lewis' hospitality in Woodruff, "The Generous Heart and Life of C. S. Lewis," published by the C. S. Lewis Institute in 2013.

12. Humphrey Carpenter explores the communal and intellectual life of C. S. Lewis and his circle in *The Inklings* (1979), highlighting how their gatherings fostered deep theological and literary discussions. In *God in the Dock* Lewis discusses the importance of Christian community and engagement with skeptics.

In *The Tech-Wise Family*, published in 2017, Andy Crouch argues that one of the most effective ways to resist the pull of screens is to cultivate embodied, communal practices that engage the senses—meals shared around a table, conversations that go beyond surface-level chatter, and rituals that connect people to something greater than themselves. When discipleship is lived out in tangible, relational ways, it becomes more compelling than the fleeting allure of entertainment.

Many believers see church as something they attend rather than a community to which they belong. Hospitality breaks down this barrier by fostering a culture where discipleship is woven into daily life rather than confined to Sunday mornings or structured programs. When Christians open their homes, they invite others into the reality of their faith—not just their polished, public selves but their ordinary lives. This authenticity is critical for spiritual growth. When people see how faith is lived out in the midst of work, parenting, suffering, and joy, they learn that discipleship is not just about intellectual knowledge but about a way of life.

Rosaria Butterfield, in *The Gospel Comes with a House Key*, recounts how her journey from atheism to Christianity was profoundly influenced by the daily life and hospitality of a Christian family who welcomed her into their home. She writes, "radically ordinary hospitality—those who live it see strangers as neighbors and neighbors as family of God... Those who live out radically ordinary hospitality see their homes not as theirs at all but as God's gift to use for the furtherance of his kingdom. They open doors; they seek out the underprivileged. They know that the gospel comes with a house key."[13] This act of inviting someone into one's life, listening to their story, and sharing the rhythms of faith serves as a compelling testimony to the truth of the gospel. "Our post-Christian neighbors need to hear and see and taste and feel authentic Christianity, hospitality spreading from every Christian home that includes neighbors in prayer, food, friendship, childcare, dog walking, and all the daily matters upon which friendships are built."[14]

To recover a biblical vision of hospitality, churches must move beyond seeing it as an occasional practice and embrace it as a core aspect of discipleship. This means encouraging believers to open their homes for meals, discussions, and shared experiences of faith. It means creating a culture where people are not afraid to show hospitality even when their

---

13. Butterfield, *The Gospel Comes with a House Key*, 11.
14. Butterfield, *The Gospel Comes with a House Key*, 95.

A DISCIPLESHIP MODEL FOR THE POST-CHRISTIAN WORLD

homes are not perfect or their schedules are busy. True hospitality is not about impressing guests but about making space for real, Christ-centered relationships to grow.

At its heart, hospitality is a reflection of the gospel itself. God, in his great love, has welcomed us into his family when we were strangers and aliens (Eph 2:19). Jesus has prepared a place for us at his table, inviting us to commune with him in the feast of his grace. When Christians practice hospitality, they mirror this divine welcome, embodying the love of Christ in tangible, everyday ways. In a world of loneliness and division, hospitality is one of the most powerful tools for making disciples, building community, and living out the radical grace of the gospel.

In this sense, the practice of hospitality is not merely an act of kindness; it is a foretaste of something far greater. When believers welcome others into their homes, they reflect the divine invitation extended to them in Christ—the invitation to join the family of God and to gather at his table. This reality finds its ultimate fulfillment in worship, where the church, as God's redeemed people, comes together to feast on his word, partake in the Lord's Supper, and experience the presence of Christ in community. Just as earthly hospitality prepares a place for others, so too does worship remind us that Jesus has prepared a place for us in his kingdom. The table of fellowship we extend in our homes is but a shadow of the greater table to which we are called—the table where discipleship culminates in the joyful worship of the triune God.

A Life Wholly Oriented Toward God

At the heart of every challenge facing discipleship today—whether cultural debates, digital distractions, or the pull toward radical individualism—is a deeper question: What ultimately shapes our desires, our loves, and our identity? The modern world offers countless competing visions of fulfillment, each demanding our allegiance. But discipleship calls us to something greater: a life wholly oriented toward God.

True discipleship is not merely about acquiring knowledge, following moral guidelines, or even engaging in community—though all these are essential. At its core, discipleship is about worship. It is about reordering our hearts to love what is truly good, beautiful, and worthy: God himself. Worship is not just one aspect of the Christian life; it is the goal of discipleship, the very reason we were created.

If discipleship is ultimately about becoming more like Christ, then it must lead us to the place where Christ himself directs us—to worship the Father in spirit and truth (John 4:24). How does worship shape our transformation? How does it combat the false narratives of the world? And how can the church recover worship as the central purpose of Christian discipleship?

Chapter 6

Worship as the Goal of Discipleship

DISCIPLESHIP IS NOT AN end in itself; it finds its fulfillment in worship. The goal of following Christ is not merely to gain knowledge, cultivate virtue, or build community—though these are all essential—but ultimately to know, love, and glorify God. If reason grounds us in truth, imagination awakens our affections, and community nurtures us in love, then corporate worship is where all these elements find their highest expression. It is in worship that we behold the glory of God, both intellectually and experientially, allowing his truth to shape our minds, his beauty to stir our hearts, and his presence to bind us together as his people. In other words, we can't disconnect discipleship from worship, the disciple from the church.

Worship is the telos of discipleship—the destination toward which every act of learning, formation, and spiritual discipline leads. Without worship, discipleship loses its ultimate purpose, becoming either a cold intellectual pursuit, an abstract aesthetic longing, or a disconnected exercise in fellowship. But when discipleship is rightly ordered toward worship, it becomes what it was always meant to be: a preparation for encountering the living God and offering him the praise, love, and devotion he is due.

Therefore, Christian discipleship is ultimately about the transformation of our entire being—mind, heart, and community—into a life of worship. The *Westminster Shorter Catechism* famously states that "Man's chief end is to glorify God and to enjoy him forever."[1] This declaration

---

1. *Westminster Shorter Catechism*, Q.1. See Lewis, *Reflections on the Psalms*, 97.

encapsulates the biblical vision of discipleship: to shape believers into people who worship God in every aspect of their lives. Worship is not an add-on to the Christian life; it is the culmination of our faith, the purpose for which we were created.

In a post-Christian age that elevates self-autonomy, entertainment, and consumerism, the call to true worship stands in stark contrast. Instead of conforming to cultural idols, discipleship reorients our hearts toward God, teaching us to love and adore him above all else. Thus, Christian discipleship is not merely about acquiring theological knowledge, modifying behavior, or participating in religious rituals—it is fundamentally about the transformation of the whole person into the image of Christ. Worship is both the means and the culmination of this transformation, shaping how believers think, love, and live. In a culture that seeks to redefine identity, manipulate desires, and fragment community, worship stands as a counterformative force that realigns our minds, reorders our affections, and reorients our entire being toward the glory of God.

Worship and the Renewal of the Mind

The renewal of the mind is central to Christian discipleship, and worship is not merely an emotional experience or a ritualistic duty; it is a formative process that reshapes how we think, perceive, and understand reality. Romans 12:2 declares, "Do not be conformed to this world, but be transformed by the renewal of your mind, that by testing you may discern what is the will of God, what is good and acceptable and perfect." In other words, worship is one of the means by which believers are reoriented from the patterns of a fallen world toward the wisdom and knowledge of God.

In a post-Christian age where cultural narratives increasingly challenge biblical truth, the renewal of the mind through worship is critical. The world catechizes people daily through media, education, entertainment, and social norms. And this catechesis happens subtly yet powerfully. Through media, we are constantly exposed to narratives that frame personal fulfillment, self-expression, and autonomy as the highest goods. Television, films, and social media curate stories where happiness is found in self-discovery rather than self-denial, where truth is subjective, and where faith is often portrayed as naïve or oppressive. The news cycle and digital platforms reinforce ideological perspectives that shape our sense of justice, ethics, and even human dignity. Without realizing it, we begin absorbing these messages, conforming to the world's patterns rather than being transformed by the renewal of our minds.

Education also plays a significant role in shaping worldview. From an early age, children and young adults are taught not only facts but frameworks for interpreting reality. Many academic institutions operate under secular assumptions, promoting naturalism, materialism, or moral relativism as intellectual norms. The idea that faith belongs to the private sphere—irrelevant to science, ethics, or public life—permeates much of modern education. Meanwhile, entertainment reinforces cultural norms about sexuality, relationships, and success, often celebrating values that stand in stark contrast to biblical teaching. Over time, these influences shape our desires, our definitions of right and wrong, and even our understanding of what it means to be human. If the church is not intentional about counter-catechizing believers through worship and discipleship, these competing voices will define how we see the world.

Worship interrupts this cycle. It is the means by which the disciple's mind is realigned to God's wisdom, trained to discern what is true, and strengthened to resist falsehood. How, then, does worship actively renew the mind, and why is this renewal so crucial for discipleship in a post-Christian age?

The Battle for the Mind in a Secular Age

Charles Taylor describes how contemporary society has created an "immanent frame," in which belief in the transcendent is not only questioned but often excluded from serious consideration.[2] The default mindset of the modern world is secular, materialistic, and self-referential, making it increasingly difficult for people to think in theological terms. Worship, however, breaks through this immanent frame by reintroducing transcendence into our thinking. When believers gather for worship, they are reminded that reality is not limited to what can be seen, measured, or scientifically analyzed—God reigns, his kingdom is advancing, and eternity is real.

---

2. The "immanent frame" is Charles Taylor's concept describing a way of understanding the world that is structured entirely within a natural, secular order, without reference to the transcendent. It is a key feature of modern secular societies, where belief in the divine becomes optional rather than assumed. Taylor contrasts this with earlier pre-modern societies, where the transcendent was deeply embedded in everyday life. See Taylor, *A Secular Age*, 539-93.

This renewal of the mind is necessary because humans do not naturally think in alignment with God's truth. Paul describes the fallen mind as "darkened in their understanding, alienated from the life of God because of the ignorance that is in them" (Eph 4:18). Sin distorts perception, leading people to embrace falsehood over truth, to rationalize sin, and to place human reason above divine revelation. Worship confronts these distortions by reordering the intellect according to God's revealed will. In song, prayer, and the preaching of Scripture, the church collectively rehearses the truths that contradict the lies of the world.

The Word of God as the Foundation for Renewal

At the center of worship is the proclamation of the word of God. The preaching and reading of Scripture are not secondary aspects of worship but the primary means by which the mind is renewed. John Calvin describes the word of God as a corrective lens that enables believers to see reality rightly: "For just as old or bleary-eyed men and those with weak vision, if you thrust before them a most beautiful book, even if they recognize it to be some sort of writing, yet can scarcely construe two words, but with the aid of spectacles will begin to read distinctly; so Scripture, gathering up the otherwise confused knowledge of God in our minds, having dispersed our dullness, clearly shows us the true God."[3]

The mind is renewed in worship when it is saturated with Scripture. This is why biblical exposition has always been central to Christian worship. The early church devoted itself to *"the apostles' teaching"* (Acts 2:42), and throughout history, church reform movements have been marked by a return to the faithful preaching of the word.

In a world where information is abundant, but wisdom is scarce, worship immerses believers in the divine wisdom of God. The reading, hearing, and meditating on Scripture in the context of worship reshapes the mind, enabling believers to reject falsehood and embrace truth.

Singing Truth into the Mind

Music is a powerful tool for renewing the mind because it engages both intellect and emotion. The Psalms demonstrate that worship through song

---

3. Calvin, *Institutes* 1.6.1.

is not merely about expressing emotion but about forming thought. Psalm 119:11 declares, "I have stored up your word in my heart, that I might not sin against you." This storing up of the word often happens through song. The melodies and lyrics of worship songs act as vehicles for theological truth, reinforcing doctrine in ways that mere instruction cannot.

Hymnody has long been a means of theological education. The Reformers understood this well—Martin Luther's hymns were designed not only to stir the heart but to teach doctrine. In the same way, Charles Wesley's hymns provided theological depth, ensuring that their worship was rooted in sound doctrine. Today, when believers sing hymns and songs that are rich in biblical truth, they are engaging in an act of discipleship that shapes how they think about God.

Colossians 3:16 highlights the importance of music in renewing the mind: "Let the word of Christ dwell in you richly, teaching and admonishing one another in all wisdom, singing psalms and hymns and spiritual songs, with thankfulness in your hearts to God." This passage connects singing with both wisdom and teaching. Worship through song is not simply an emotional exercise but an intellectual one—it implants the word of Christ deeply within the mind. This is why the content of worship music matters. Songs that are biblically rich and theologically sound play a crucial role in shaping a believer's understanding of God, while shallow or theologically deficient songs fail to nourish the mind.

Prayer and the Renewal of Thought

Prayer, as a means of grace, is also a means through which God renews the minds of his people. The Westminster Standards affirm that prayer, along with the word and sacraments, is a primary channel by which God strengthens and sanctifies believers, shaping their hearts and minds to conform to his will. Prayer is not merely an act of communication with God; it is a formative practice through which the mind is reshaped, anxieties are surrendered, and faith is strengthened.

Philippians 4:6-7 further reinforces this connection between prayer and the renewal of thought, stating, "Do not be anxious about anything, but in everything by prayer and supplication with thanksgiving let your requests be made known to God. And the peace of God, which surpasses all understanding, will guard your hearts and your minds in Christ Jesus." Here, Paul presents prayer as the means by which God reorients human thought away from fear and anxiety toward divine peace. In a world filled with distractions, uncertainties, and pressures, prayer serves as the regular practice by which believers refocus their minds on God's sovereignty and faithfulness. This renewal is not simply a psychological exercise but a spiritual work of grace, wherein God grants his people the ability to see reality through the lens of faith rather than through the distortions of sin and worry.

In the life of discipleship, this renewal of the mind through prayer is essential. Just as the word of God instructs and the sacraments confirm our participation in Christ, prayer serves as a continual realignment of our thoughts and desires toward God's truth. Left to ourselves, our minds easily drift into patterns of self-reliance, doubt, or even despair, but prayer brings us back into active dependence on God. Through prayer, believers internalize the truths of Scripture, develop spiritual discernment, and cultivate a posture of trust rather than anxiety.

In corporate worship, this takes on an even greater significance, as the gathered church lifts its collective voice in prayer, reinforcing its shared faith and dependence on God's grace. This is why prayer must remain central in both personal and corporate discipleship. It is not an optional discipline but an essential practice through which believers experience the ongoing renewal of their minds. The very act of prayer reorders priorities, reminds disciples of their identity in Christ, and equips them to live faithfully in a world that seeks to conform them to lesser things. As a means of grace, prayer does not merely express faith—it strengthens and sustains it, ensuring that discipleship is not a static process but a dynamic journey of continual transformation into the image of Christ.

Worship and the Reordering of the Heart

While worship renews the mind by aligning our thoughts with God's truth, it also does something deeper—it reorders our hearts. Discipleship is not merely about knowing what is true but loving what is good. Our greatest problem is not just incorrect thinking but disordered affections. We often love the wrong things too much and the right things too little, allowing lesser desires to take the place of God. Worship, then, is not only an intellectual exercise but a formative encounter that reshapes what we treasure most. It redirects our desires from the fleeting idols of this world to the eternal beauty of God. If discipleship is about learning to love God with all our heart, soul, and strength, then worship is the means by which our affections are trained and properly ordered. But how does worship accomplish this? And why is the reordering of the heart so crucial in a culture that constantly competes for our love and loyalty.

Scripture consistently portrays the heart as the wellspring of life (Prov 4:23), the seat of human love, longing, and devotion. The fundamental problem of sin is not just a failure to think rightly but a disordering of what we love most. Since the fall, human beings have sought fulfillment in things other than God. Restlessness is the hallmark of a heart that is misaligned, longing for satisfaction yet unable to find it in the fleeting idols of the world. Idolatry is not merely an ancient phenomenon; it is the persistent condition of the human soul, manifesting in new forms in every generation. As Calvin observed, "man's nature, so to speak, is a perpetual factory of idols."[4] The human heart is not neutral—it is always in a state of worship, always loving something supremely.

The world fights for our affections by constantly placing before us counterfeit loves—things that promise fulfillment yet leave us empty. Consumer culture, for example, conditions us to believe that our worth is found in what we own, subtly forming us into people who see material success as the highest good. Advertisements are not just selling products; they are shaping desires, persuading us that we will only be happy if we have more, look better, or achieve greater recognition. Social media cultivates a hunger for approval, teaching us to seek validation through likes, shares, and curated personas rather than in the unshakable love of God. Entertainment and digital distraction numb our hearts, offering a constant stream of content designed to keep us engaged, entertained, and ultimately dependent. Even good things—family, career, relationships—can become disordered loves when they take the place of God, demanding our ultimate devotion. In a world that continually misdirects our desires, worship stands as an act of resistance, a reorientation of the heart toward its true fulfillment in Christ. If we are not intentional about training our affections through discipleship and worship, the culture will train them for us.

As Paul states in Romans 1:25, fallen humanity has "exchanged the truth about God for a lie and worshiped and served the creature rather than the Creator." The result is not only a distortion of belief but a corruption of desire. When something other than God holds ultimate value in a person's life—whether wealth, status, relationships, personal autonomy, or ideological causes—that thing becomes an idol, shaping identity, purpose, and hope

---

4. Calvin, *Institutes*, 1.2.8.

in ways that can never truly satisfy. The fundamental issue, then, is not just that people *believe* falsehoods but that they *love* wrongly.

Therefore, discipleship is not only about intellectual formation but about the reformation of desire. As Augustine writes, "You have made us for yourself, O Lord, and our heart is restless until it rests in you."[5] This restlessness is a symptom of hearts longing for God but seeking fulfillment in substitutes that ultimately leave them empty. The challenge of Christian discipleship is to redirect those desires toward their proper end—loving God above all else.

This is why true worship is not just about expressing devotion but about being transformed in the presence of God. If false worship leads to disordered affections, true worship reorients them. When the church gathers to worship God, it is not simply performing a religious duty; it is engaging in the most formative practice of the Christian life. In worship, believers are invited to behold the beauty of the Lord (Ps 27:4), to delight in him above all else (Ps 37:4), and to have their desires recalibrated by His truth and goodness. Worship retrains the heart, teaching it what is truly worthy of love. As disciples learn to treasure Christ above all else, they begin to experience the freedom that comes from loving rightly—the freedom of finding their greatest joy in the One who alone can satisfy.

Worship as the Cure for Idolatry

Biblical worship, therefore, is a form of heart-rehabilitation. Christian worship functions as a counter-liturgy against the false liturgies of the world. Every culture has its own "liturgies"—practices and habits that shape desires in ways that compete with the love of God. The mall, the smartphone, the university, the political rally—each has its own rituals that train people in a particular vision of the good life. The consumeristic liturgy teaches that personal fulfillment comes from acquiring more possessions. The digital liturgy conditions people to crave constant validation. The political liturgy fosters an identity rooted in tribal allegiance rather than the kingdom of God. These secular liturgies shape the heart's desires in ways that often go unnoticed.

Christian worship, however, re-forms the heart by directing its deepest longings toward the only one who can truly satisfy. The practices of gathered worship—singing, prayer, confession, communion—are not

---

5. Augustine, *Confessions* 1.1.

empty traditions but means of grace through which God reshapes what we love. In corporate worship, believers are invited to dethrone the false gods that have captivated their hearts and to enthrone Christ as Lord. The songs we sing, the Scriptures we read, the prayers we pray—each element of worship is designed to pull the affections away from self-centered desires and toward God-centered devotion.

The Psalms provide a powerful example of how worship reorders the heart. Psalm 73 illustrates the struggle of a believer whose heart had been led astray. The psalmist confesses that he envied the prosperity of the wicked and felt that his devotion to God was in vain. But everything changed when he entered the sanctuary of God: "But when I thought how to understand this, it seemed to me a wearisome task, until I went into the sanctuary of God; then I discerned their end" (Ps 73:16-17). The act of worship opened his eyes, shifting his perspective and reorienting his desires. By encountering God in worship, he was freed from the idolatry of comparison and restored to a place of trust and joy in God alone.

Worship as a School of Love

Jesus taught that the greatest commandment is to love the Lord with all one's heart, soul, and mind (Matt 22:37). But love is not merely an abstract concept; it is something that must be cultivated through practice. Worship serves as the training ground where believers learn to love God rightly. In this sense, Christian discipleship finds its core in worship, serving as the training ground where God reshapes and refines the hearts of His people.[6] In other words, at its essence, discipleship involves a lifelong journey of becoming more like Christ and growing in spiritual maturity. It involves the process of surrendering old ways and allowing God to mold individuals into the image of His Son.

Corporate worship, within this context, transcends mere routine or ritual; it is a dynamic encounter with God that shapes and molds hearts. James Smith's analogy of worship as a "gymnasium" captures the idea of intentional and disciplined training. In worship, participants engage in exercises of praise, prayer, confession, and thanksgiving, which stretch and strengthen spiritual muscles. Through sincere and open participation in worship, God meets individuals in this sacred space, challenging perspectives, transforming desires, and cultivating a heart aligned with his.

---

6. Smith, *You Are What You Love*, 77.

As we gather to worship, God retrains hearts by realigning affections and priorities, fostering a recognition of his authority and goodness. Moments of worship become encounters with the beauty and majesty of God, stirring a love for him and a desire to follow him closely. Hearts are softened, and wills are submitted as individuals pour out their hearts in worship. God responds with grace, mercy, and transforming power, instilling a sense of belonging and purpose as cherished disciples. Through continued participation in this formative practice, discipleship deepens, relationships with God grow, and lives align with his purposes.

Consider the role of the sacraments in shaping and sustaining the life of discipleship. Baptism is not merely a ritual or a symbolic gesture; it is a deeply formative act that marks the believer's initiation into the covenant community of faith. It is a visible sign and seal of God's promise, testifying that salvation is by grace alone through faith alone in Christ alone. Baptism signifies a decisive break from the old life of sin and entrance into the new life in Christ, uniting believers with his death and resurrection (Rom 6:3-4). As a corporate act, baptism also reminds the church that faith is not an isolated journey but a shared reality within the body of Christ. It shapes the believer's identity, reinforcing that they are no longer defined by the world's shifting narratives of self-construction but by their union with Christ. Through baptism, discipleship is rooted in the reality that our truest identity is found not in personal achievement or cultural affirmation, but in belonging to Christ and his church.

The Lord's Supper, likewise, is far more than a memorial meal; it is a repeated, tangible participation in the grace of God. When believers gather around the Lord's Table, they are not merely recalling an event from the distant past, but actively communing with the risen Christ, who nourishes his people with himself. Jesus declared, "Whoever feeds on my flesh and drinks my blood abides in me, and I in him" (John 6:56). The Eucharist (or Communion) reorients our desires by reminding us that our deepest hunger can only be satisfied in Christ. In a world that constantly tempts us to seek fulfillment in fleeting pleasures, the Lord's Supper calls us back to the source of true life. It is in this sacred meal that the church learns dependence, trust, and the rhythm of continual renewal. As disciples participate in the body and blood of Christ by faith, they are strengthened for the journey of faith, sustained by the very life of their Savior.

These embodied acts of worship—baptism and the Lord's Supper—are essential for forming believers into people who love and trust God. In a culture that often reduces faith to intellectual assent or personal spirituality, the sacraments provide a holistic vision of discipleship that engages both body and soul. They teach us that faith is not simply about knowing the right doctrines, nor is it about individualistic experiences—it is about belonging to a redeemed people, being nourished by the grace of God, and living in the reality of Christ's kingdom. Through these sacred practices, discipleship is continually shaped by the gospel, reminding us that our identity, sustenance, and ultimate hope are found in Christ alone. Worship, then, is not just the culmination of discipleship, but its ongoing rhythm—a pattern of grace that shapes us into the image of the one we worship.

Corporate worship also fosters humility, which is essential for reordering the heart. In confession, believers acknowledge their sin and receive God's mercy. In singing psalms and hymns, they lift their voices in submission to God's truth. In listening to the word preached, they are confronted with God's reality, correcting the distortions of their own hearts. Worship teaches believers to love what is good, to reject what is evil, and to long for what is eternal.

Worship and the Joy of True Satisfaction

The ultimate goal of worship is not simply to correct wrong desires but to lead believers into the joy of true satisfaction in God. Psalm 16:11 declares, "You make known to me the path of life; in your presence there is fullness of joy; at your right hand are pleasures forevermore." Worship is not a burden; it is the fulfillment of the heart's deepest longing. The reason sin is so enticing is that it promises joy apart from God. But these promises are empty. The world's pleasures fade, its idols disappoint, and its philosophies shift with the times. Only God is unchanging, and only he can provide the lasting joy that every heart seeks. Only in his presence we find pleasures forevermore.

This is why worship is not merely a duty but a delight. As believers grow in discipleship, they move from seeing worship as an obligation to experiencing it as a joy. The more they behold the beauty of Christ, the less they are drawn to the counterfeit joys of the world. Worship is the process by which the soul is weaned off lesser loves and enraptured by the supreme love of God. And since it is a process, the reordering of the heart is not a one-time event but a lifelong journey. Every day, the world presents new idols, new distractions, and new temptations that seek to pull the heart away from God. This is why regular, intentional worship is essential. There is not discipleship detached from the life of the church. Weekly corporate worship is not an optional gathering but a vital practice that anchors believers in God's reality.

Ultimately, the goal of worship is not only to reorder the heart but to prepare believers for eternity. In the new creation, worship will no longer be hindered by sin or distraction. The redeemed will see God face to face and love him perfectly. Until that day, worship remains the means by which the heart is continually turned from idols to the living God. In worship, discipleship finds its highest expression, for to worship God rightly is to love him fully—and that is the ultimate purpose for which we were created.

Worship in a Digital Age: The Need for Embodied Discipleship

If worship is meant to renew our minds (reason) and reorder our hearts (imagination), shaping our deepest loves and desires, then the way we worship matters. Worship is not merely about personal reflection or individual expression—it is a communal and embodied act. Yet, in a world increasingly dominated by digital interactions, virtual experiences, and disembodied relationships, the very nature of worship is being reshaped. In an age where screens mediate much of life, from relationships to entertainment to learning, many are tempted to view worship as just another content stream—something to be consumed rather than participated in.

The world isolates us by redefining community as something that can be experienced passively and from a distance. Social media platforms, while promising connection, often foster superficial relationships where curated personas replace genuine vulnerability. The rise of remote work, on-demand entertainment, and digital communication has made it easier than ever to structure life around personal convenience rather than communal engagement. Even within churches, live-streamed services and virtual interactions—while valuable in certain contexts—can subtly erode the habit of gathering in person, making physical presence feel optional rather than essential. Meanwhile, cultural narratives of radical individualism encourage people to prioritize self-expression and autonomy over commitment to a shared life with others. The result is a deep but often unrecognized loneliness, where people are surrounded by digital noise but lack the embodied presence of others who truly know them. Worship, however, calls us back to something deeper—an act that cannot be reduced to a solitary experience but must be lived out in community, where we sing, pray, and partake of the sacraments together as the body of Christ.

But how can discipleship thrive when so much of life is shifting toward digital spaces? And what does it mean to reclaim embodied worship in a culture that increasingly disconnects faith from physical presence? In an age of increasing isolation, the church must not only preach about community but actively cultivate spaces where believers practice belonging, presence, and shared life.

Christian discipleship is not meant to be a purely intellectual or private endeavor; it is a holistic process that involves the whole person—body and soul. The Scriptures do not portray faith as something that exists only in the realm of ideas but as something lived out in the physical, communal reality of the church. When Jesus called his disciples, he did not invite them into an abstract philosophy but into a way of life that involved walking with him, eating with him, and learning from him in embodied presence. The Incarnation itself—the eternal Word becoming flesh—testifies that faith cannot be separated from physical, tangible reality (John 1:14). In contrast, much of modern life is increasingly disembodied, reducing relationships, learning, and even worship to digital interfaces rather than real, incarnate participation.

The Limits of Virtual Worship and AI-Driven Discipleship

The modern reliance on digital platforms for worship, while convenient, can distort the very nature of Christian formation. Virtual services, while beneficial in times of necessity, cannot replace the physical gathering of believers. Worship is not merely about consuming religious content but about participating in the life of the body of Christ. When believers worship through a screen, they miss the full depth of communal engagement—the shared singing, the corporate prayers, the physical gestures of worship, and the sacramental life of the church. Virtual worship lacks the formative power of these physical and relational interactions.

Even more concerning is the emergence of artificial intelligence in religious spaces. AI-generated sermons, chatbots for spiritual guidance, and algorithm-driven religious experiences raise profound theological and ethical concerns. AI may provide theological information, but it cannot shepherd souls. It lacks the ability to empathize, to challenge, to guide believers in relational growth. The personal, relational aspect of discipleship cannot be replicated by technology. True spiritual formation requires real presence, the kind that can only happen through human relationships in the context of community.

Embodied Worship in a Disembodied Age

In an age of digital isolation and hyper-individualism, the act of physically gathering for worship and discipleship is a radical and countercultural practice. The church, by its very nature, is a community of embodied believers who gather together as the people of God. The New Testament assumes this kind of physical presence, as seen in Hebrews 10:24–25: "And let us consider how to stir up one another to love and good works, not neglecting to meet together, as is the habit of some, but encouraging one another." The church is not a collection of isolated individuals but a gathered people who worship, serve, and grow together in Christ.

Embodied worship confronts the fragmentation of modern life by reorienting believers toward shared presence and communal participation. In a culture where people are conditioned to be consumers—passively watching rather than actively engaging—worship demands full participation. It requires standing, kneeling, lifting hands, confessing, receiving the Eucharist, and singing together with one voice. These actions are not incidental; they shape the worshiper's affections and deepen the reality of faith. The reality is that liturgies, whether secular or sacred, train our hearts through repeated actions. In this sense, the church's liturgical practices counteract the formative power of digital consumerism, drawing believers into a worship that is not passive but transformative.

The church must call people not merely to know about God but to encounter him in the fullness of worship. The church must invite people not only to know that God is good but to taste and see that he is good (Ps 34:8). This means that discipleship should always lead back to corporate worship. Teaching believers theology should not be for the sake of intellectual pride but for the deepening of worship. Encouraging spiritual disciplines should not be about self-improvement but about fostering a heart that delights in God. Discipleship, at its core, is about forming people whose entire lives become an offering of worship to the Lord (Rom 12:1).

Worship as the Culmination of Discipleship

It is evident, then, that discipleship is not an end in itself but a journey leading to the highest purpose of human existence—worship, because the God the Father is seeking true worshipers (John 4:24). Therefore, true discipleship is not simply about gaining knowledge, cultivating virtue, or participating in religious practices. While these elements are essential, they serve a greater purpose: to glorify and enjoy God forever. Worship is the culmination of discipleship because it brings every aspect of spiritual formation—reason, imagination, and community—into their proper alignment with God. In worship, the disciple's intellect is engaged with divine truth, the heart is stirred with holy desire, and the community is united in joyful adoration. All growth in faith, all pursuit of wisdom, and all acts of obedience ultimately find their fulfillment in the worship of God, who alone is worthy of our highest love and devotion.

Therefore, the goal of discipleship is not self-improvement or intellectual mastery but a life wholly oriented toward God. Scripture teaches that human beings were created for worship. The first commandment—"You shall have no other gods before me" (Exod 20:3)—reminds us that idolatry is the greatest hindrance to true worship. As fallen creatures, we are prone to misdirect our worship, placing our highest affections in things that cannot satisfy—money, power, relationships, entertainment, or self-fulfillment. This is why discipleship must ultimately lead to the reordering of desires so that God is rightly enthroned in the heart. Discipleship leads to worship, and worship is not just an isolated act; it is a way of life in which the whole person—body, mind, and soul—is continually offered to God.

John Piper famously stated, "Missions exists because worship doesn't," emphasizing that the ultimate goal of evangelism and discipleship is to bring people into the worship of God. Discipleship that remains solely focused on acquiring theological knowledge or cultivating moral behavior, yet does not lead to adoration and communion with the triune God, falls short of its true purpose. Authentic formation is not complete until it awakens a heart that delights in God, exalts him in worship, and finds its deepest satisfaction in his presence. This is why, as Calvin declared, the disciple must ultimately say, "I offer my heart to you, O Lord, promptly and sincerely."

Worship as the End of Human Longing

Worship is the fulfillment of the deepest human desires. Throughout history, philosophers and theologians have recognized that people long for something beyond themselves. Every human being is searching for meaning, for joy, for something that will satisfy the soul's deepest hunger. The secular world offers countless substitutes—career, relationships, entertainment, political ideologies—but all of these ultimately fall short.

Discipleship, then, is about training the affections and imagination—helping believers see that what they truly long for is not found in the temporary pleasures of the world but in the eternal joy of knowing and worshiping God. The church must cultivate this vision of worship, helping people move beyond a shallow, consumer-driven faith to a deep, soul-satisfying delight in the glory of God.

The Church as a Worshiping Community

Because worship is the culmination of discipleship, the church is called to be a worshiping community. The gathered worship of the church is not just a weekly event but the heartbeat of Christian life. In worship, believers are reminded of their true identity as God's people, reoriented toward eternal realities, and strengthened for the journey of discipleship. Worship is not an individualistic endeavor but a communal act in which believers exhort one another, confess their faith together, and participate in the sacraments that nourish the soul (Heb 10:24–25).

Throughout Scripture, corporate worship is seen as the defining mark of God's people. In the Old Testament, Israel was called to be a worshiping nation, centered around the temple and the sacrifices that pointed forward to Christ. In the New Testament, the early church gathered regularly for the apostles' teaching, the breaking of bread, prayer, and fellowship (Acts 2:42). The heavenly vision of Revelation presents the church's ultimate destiny as eternal worship, with people from every tribe and tongue crying out, "Worthy is the Lamb who was slain!" (Rev 5:12).

Therefore, worship is not only the culmination of discipleship but also its driving force. A church that truly worships will inevitably cultivate mature disciples, who in turn will bear witness to Christ in both word and deed. Worship shapes believers, reorienting their hearts toward God and compelling them to live in obedience, love, and service. It is in the presence of God that disciples are formed, renewed, and sent out to reflect his glory in the world.

This rhythm of worship and discipleship should define the life of the church. Corporate worship is not an isolated event but the wellspring from which disciples are shaped and sent into the world. When believers gather to glorify God, they are being formed into the likeness of Christ—challenged by his word, nourished by his grace, and strengthened in faith. Worship fuels discipleship, and discipleship, in turn, deepens and enriches worship.

The Eternal Worship of God's People

Ultimately, worship is not merely the goal of discipleship in this life—it is the purpose for which we were created for all eternity. The story of Scripture does not end with human achievement, cultural transformation, or even personal sanctification, but with the people of God dwelling in his presence and worshiping him forever. Revelation's final vision (Rev 21–22) unveils a renewed creation where every tear is wiped away, every longing is fulfilled, and every heart is caught up in unhindered adoration of the one who made all things new. This is the culmination of history, not as a conclusion but as the beginning of eternal joy.

Jonathan Edwards, reflecting on this eternal reality, wrote: "The enjoyment of [God] is the only happiness with which our souls can be satisfied. Fathers and mothers, husbands, wives, or children, or the company of earthly friends, are but shadows; but the enjoyment of God is the substance. These are but scattered beams, but God is the sun. These are but streams, but God is the fountain. These are but drops, but God is the ocean."[7] If this is our eternal destiny, then discipleship must always be about preparing believers for that final worship. The church's mission is not simply to help people navigate the challenges of modern life but to awaken in them a hunger for God, a longing to see him face to face, and a life oriented toward the worship that will never end.

Worship, then, is both the foundation and the culmination of discipleship. It is not an afterthought or an optional expression of faith—it is the very essence of what it means to follow Christ. Every aspect of Christian formation—learning, serving, growing in holiness—is incomplete until it leads to worship, a wholehearted, joyful, Christ-exalting offering of our entire selves to God. As Lewis observes, "the Church exists for nothing else

---

7. Edwards, "The Christian Pilgrim," 244.

but to draw men into Christ, to make them little Christs. If they are not doing that, all the cathedrals, clergy, missions, sermons, even the Bible itself, are simply a waste of time. God became Man for no other purpose."[8] And the call of Psalm 95:6 rings true for every generation: "Oh come, let us worship and bow down; let us kneel before the Lord, our Maker!"

In worship, we find our true purpose, our deepest joy, and the fulfillment of all we were created to be. Worship is the place where reason, imagination, and community find their highest expression. Through reason, worship engages the intellect, grounding believers in the unshakable truth of God's character and redemptive work. It cultivates a faith that is not only spiritually alive but intellectually robust, shaping minds to see reality as God has revealed it. Through imagination, worship stirs the deepest longings of the heart, drawing disciples into the beauty, wonder, and mystery of God's presence. It satisfies the soul's restless search for meaning and transforms desire toward its true fulfillment. Through community, worship unites believers as one body, forming them through shared rhythms of prayer, praise, and sacramental life.

Lewis's vision of discipleship reminds us that faith is not merely about acquiring knowledge, adhering to doctrine, or even defending truth—it is about learning to see rightly, love rightly, and belong rightly to the people of God. Worship is where the mind is renewed, the heart is reoriented, and the people of God are shaped for the life of the kingdom.

---

8. Lewis, *Mere Christianity*, 171.

Chapter 7

Bringing It All Together

DISCIPLESHIP IS NOT AN event, a class, or a program; it is a lifelong journey of being shaped into the image of Christ. It is the call to leave behind an old way of life and embrace a new identity in Christ, allowing every part of our being—our thoughts, desires, and relationships—to be transformed by his grace. When Jesus invited his followers with the simple yet profound words, "Follow me," he was not offering an optional path for the spiritually inclined. He was summoning men and women into the very heart of God's mission, a life defined by faith, obedience, and transformation.

At the core of this journey is the call to love the Lord our God with all our heart, soul, mind, and strength. True discipleship does not simply equip believers with knowledge, nor does it merely demand outward conformity to Christian ethics. It seeks to engage the whole person, reshaping how we think, what we love, and how we live in community. This holistic vision of discipleship is not just a response to Christ's command in the Great Commission; it is the means by which believers grow into maturity, living as a faithful witness in a world desperately in need of truth and grace.

The challenges of modern discipleship are significant. The cultural landscape has shifted dramatically, presenting new obstacles to faith formation. In an era marked by intellectual skepticism, many struggle to see Christianity as rational or credible. At the same time, widespread spiritual apathy dulls the hunger for God, making faith seem irrelevant in a world filled with distractions. Even for those who are drawn to Christianity, the deeply individualistic ethos of modern society makes it difficult to cultivate the kind of rich, communal faith that has historically sustained the church.

Yet, despite these challenges, the call to discipleship remains unchanged. The task before us is not to reinvent Christianity to make it more palatable, nor to retreat from the world in despair. Rather, it is to recover a discipleship that is deeply rooted in truth, awakened by beauty, and sustained by community. As we seek to form whole disciples, we must, by the power and grace of the Holy Spirit, renew the mind, awaken the heart, and restore the essential role of relationships in shaping faith. But how does this take shape in the life of the church? How can reason, imagination, and community work together in a discipleship model that is both faithful and transformative? What does it look like to tie these elements together into a holistic vision of Christian formation?

Discipleship of the Mind: Cultivating Intellectual Depth

For many in the modern world, faith and reason seem like opposing forces. The assumption that Christianity is irrational has taken deep root in secular culture, leading many to dismiss it without serious consideration. The rise of scientific materialism, the influence of relativism, and the aggressive critiques of the New Atheists have fostered an intellectual climate in which belief in God is often seen as naïve or outdated. This cultural shift has left many Christians unprepared to engage with skepticism, and as a result, faith is often presented as a purely emotional or moral commitment rather than as a rationally compelling worldview.

Yet, Christianity has always been a faith that demands the engagement of the mind. The Scriptures repeatedly call believers to seek wisdom (Prov 4:7), to meditate on God's law (Ps 1:2), and to be transformed by the renewing of their thinking (Rom 12:2). Jesus himself commanded his followers to love God with all their mind (Mark 12:30), making intellectual formation a vital aspect of discipleship. Throughout church history, great Christian thinkers such as Augustine, Aquinas, Pascal, and Lewis have demonstrated that faith and reason are not enemies but allies, each deepening the other.

The life and writings of C. S. Lewis serve as a model for intellectual discipleship in a skeptical age. Lewis did not merely argue for Christianity—he illuminated its coherence, beauty, and explanatory power. He understood that belief in God was not only reasonable but necessary for making sense of reality, morality, and human longing. His work engaged deeply with philosophy, literature, and theology, showing that Christianity offers a far more compelling vision of life than its secular alternatives. In an age where many assume that faith is opposed to logic, Lewis demonstrated that Christianity not only withstands intellectual scrutiny but provides the most rational foundation for truth, meaning, and morality.

A renewed discipleship of the mind must take seriously the need for theological depth and critical thinking. Christians must be equipped to wrestle with difficult questions, engage with opposing viewpoints, and articulate their faith with clarity and confidence. The church must recover the lost art of intellectual hospitality, where doubts are welcomed, hard questions are explored, and the pursuit of truth is encouraged. A faith that fears questions is a faith that will not endure, but a faith that seeks understanding will be one that grows stronger over time.

Churches can implement this by incorporating apologetics and worldview training into their discipleship programs. Study groups that explore *Mere Christianity* alongside Scripture, book discussions on *Confessions* or contemporary cultural critiques, and courses on the historical, philosophical, and rational foundations of the faith can equip believers to engage their culture thoughtfully. Preaching, too, should not shy away from theological depth but should model rigorous engagement with Scripture and the Christian tradition—demonstrating how faith makes sense of the world we live in.

Yet, discipleship of the mind is not about amassing theological knowledge for its own sake. It is about seeing reality rightly and aligning our thoughts with the truth of God's word. A disciple whose mind is renewed by truth will not only be equipped to withstand intellectual challenges but will also develop a deeper love for God and a greater ability to proclaim the gospel to a world in need.

Discipleship of the Heart: Awakening Spiritual Affections

If the modern world presents intellectual challenges to faith, it presents even greater challenges to the affections. The relentless pursuit of entertainment, achievement, and self-fulfillment has dulled the deeper longings of the soul, replacing the hunger for God with the pursuit of lesser joys. In an age where distraction is the norm, the still, small voice of God is easily drowned out by the noise of everyday life. The result is often a thin, therapeutic faith that provides emotional comfort but lacks transformative power.

Christianity, however, is not merely a set of intellectual propositions; it is a vision of life that captivates the heart. True discipleship must go beyond knowledge and awaken desire—desire for holiness, for beauty, and for the presence of God. This is why Jesus did not simply instruct his followers in doctrine; he captured their imaginations, spoke in parables, and invited them into a life that was richer and fuller than anything they had known. The gospel is not merely something to be understood; it is something to be *loved*.

Lewis understood the importance of engaging the imagination in discipleship. He recognized that before people embrace Christianity as true, they must first sense that it is good and beautiful. Through his fiction, essays, and reflections, he showed that the gospel is not just a doctrine to accept but a reality to be experienced. His works invite readers to see the world through a new lens, stirring a longing for something beyond the material and awakening the desire for a joy that nothing in this world can fully satisfy—what he called *sehnsucht*, or the "inconsolable longing" that points to God.

Discipleship that fails to engage the heart will always fall short. The church must recover a vision of Christian formation that awakens love for Christ, cultivates spiritual disciplines, and nurtures deep, soul-satisfying worship. It must provide spaces where believers can encounter the living God—not just through study but through beauty, silence, prayer, and awe. A disciple whose heart is captivated by the glory of God will not be easily swayed by the distractions of the world, for their deepest affections will be rooted in something far greater.

This happens through the arts, storytelling, liturgy, and the creative expression of faith. Churches should embrace literature, music, poetry, and visual art that reflect the beauty and mystery of God's truth. Reading and discussing works like *The Chronicles of Narnia* or *The Great Divorce* can open imaginative doors into theological truths in ways that arguments alone cannot. Worship services should not be reduced to intellectual exercises but should invite awe and wonder—through rich hymnody, reflective silence, sacred space, and the rhythm of liturgical practices.

The imagination is also shaped through *experience*. Fasting, retreats, and encounters with nature serve to remind us that faith is not abstract but embodied and real. Helping believers develop habits of wonder—whether through creation, creative disciplines, or meaningful silence—can stir a hunger for God that sustains them far beyond intellectual assent. Lewis understood this well; his work testifies that discipleship is not only about what we *believe*, but also about what we *love* and *long for*.

Discipleship in Community: Forming Relationships of Grace

Discipleship is not meant to be a solitary endeavor. From the very beginning, God designed faith to be formed in community. As Lewis observed, the Christian life is not one of isolation but of fellowship. The church is not merely a gathering of like-minded individuals; it is the body of Christ, a family of believers united in love. Throughout Scripture, we see that faith is passed down and sustained through relationships—through mentorship, friendship, and shared life. The early church thrived not because of programs or buildings, but because believers devoted themselves to one another, walking together in truth and love.

Yet, modern discipleship often struggles to foster deep community. The individualism of contemporary culture has crept into the church, making faith a private journey rather than a shared pilgrimage. Many believers attend church anonymously, without being truly known, and as a result, discipleship becomes an isolated effort rather than a communal transformation. In such environments, *Moralistic Therapeutic Deism* thrives, because there is little accountability, little suffering shared, and little vulnerability. But discipleship requires relationship. Growth in Christ happens not in a vacuum, but in the messy, beautiful, Spirit-filled life of the church.

The life of C. S. Lewis illustrates the power of Christian friendship in shaping faith. His circle of friends—especially the Inklings—was not just a forum for literary critique but a community of spiritual sharpening. These relationships were marked by intellectual engagement, deep affection, and mutual encouragement. Lewis's own journey of faith was profoundly influenced by such friendships, reminding us that discipleship is best cultivated through meaningful, grace-filled relationships. As Proverbs says, "Iron sharpens iron, and one man sharpens another" (Prov 27:17).

A church committed to whole-person discipleship must intentionally create environments where believers walk alongside one another. Faith is not only taught in classrooms; it is forged in shared life—in living rooms, over dinner tables, through prayer and laughter and confession. Churches must prioritize small groups and discipleship communities that go beyond curriculum and into authentic relationships. These should be places where believers are known, loved, challenged, and encouraged. Intergenerational discipleship should be normalized—pairing younger believers with older mentors who can pass on wisdom and model spiritual maturity.

This also means recovering the sacred practice of *hospitality*—not simply entertaining guests, but opening homes and lives in vulnerability and welcome. Meals shared around tables, not just programs in church buildings, are often where the deepest transformation takes place. Churches must cultivate cultures of grace, where questions are welcomed, failures are forgiven, and Christ is seen in one another. When community is rich and Christ-centered, discipleship becomes less about attending events and more about becoming a people—a people shaped by grace and sent into the world with love.

Worship and Discipleship

All of these elements—reason, imagination, and community—find their fulfillment and orientation in *worship*. The ultimate goal of discipleship is not merely to know more or behave better, but to lead people into deeper communion with the living God—to glorify him with their entire being. At its heart, discipleship is about rightly ordered love: loving God above all else, and from that love, living a life that reflects his character and purposes. Worship is both the fuel and the end of this journey.

From the beginning, humanity was created for worship. In the garden of Eden, Adam and Eve walked in perfect fellowship with their Creator, delighting in his presence and living in harmony with his will. Sin fractured this relationship, redirecting our worship toward created things rather than the Creator (Rom 1:25). Every false pursuit, every misplaced affection, every fractured identity can be traced back to this misdirection of worship—a soul oriented away from God. The story of redemption is, in essence, a story of reorientation: God calling his people back to himself through covenant, rescue, and restoration.

Jesus, the true and perfect image of God, came to restore what was lost. His life was one of constant communion with the Father, and by his death and resurrection, he invites us into that same communion. The call to discipleship is, at its core, a call to worship—a summons to re-center our lives on the glory of God and to participate in the life of the triune God. This is why Jesus declared the greatest commandment to be the love of God with all our heart, soul, mind, and strength (Mark 12:30). It is the very definition of discipleship.

Therefore, the practices of corporate worship—word and sacrament, confession and assurance, song and silence—are not tangential to discipleship; they *are* discipleship. Worship trains the mind to dwell on truth, the heart to desire what is holy, and the community to love and forgive one another. It is in worship that believers are re-storied—reminded of who God is, who they are, and what the gospel means for their everyday lives. In a fragmented and distracted world, worship forms us slowly, deeply, and beautifully into the likeness of Christ.

A Call to Action

If the church is to remain faithful and fruitful in a post-Christian, post-truth world, it must recover and reimagine discipleship as formation—not merely as information transfer or behavioral modification, but as the shaping of the whole person in Christ. This will not happen accidentally. It requires intention, investment, and a renewed commitment to walking with others over time. It requires resisting cultural patterns of isolation, distraction, and shallow belief. And it requires re-centering the life of the church on the love of God and the joy of being his people.

Churches must develop a culture where discipleship is the priority, not just one of many programs. Leaders must be formed not just to teach, but to model life with God. Parents must be equipped to disciple their children. Worship must be rooted in Scripture and oriented toward the glory of God. Communities must be built where believers are known, challenged, and encouraged to grow. The work is slow. The fruit is gradual. But the outcome is a people who are resilient in faith, radiant in love, and ready to witness to the world—not with fear or compromise, but with courage and joy.

This is the kind of discipleship modeled by C. S. Lewis. It is thoughtful, imaginative, relational, and worshipful. It is the kind of discipleship the early church embodied in the face of a hostile world. And it is the kind of discipleship that the church today must recover if it is to stand as a light in the darkness. The invitation of Jesus—*Follow me*—is not just a call to believe. It is a call to become. To become people who love what is true, desire what is beautiful, live what is good, and worship the one who is all in all.

So let us take up this call. Let us train our minds in the truth of God's word. Let us stir our hearts to long for his presence. Let us walk together in grace-filled community. And let us offer our whole lives—body and soul, heart and mind—as living sacrifices, holy and pleasing to God. This is our spiritual worship. This is the way of Christ. This is the journey of true discipleship.

Bibliography

Anselm. *Proslogion*. Notre Dame: University of Notre Dame Press, 1965.
Barrett, William. *Irrational Man: A Study in Existential Philosophy*. New York: Anchor Books, 1990.
Benedict, Ruth. *Patterns of Culture*. Boston: Houghton Mifflin, 1934.
Boas, Franz. *The Mind of Primitive Man*. New York: Macmillan, 1911.
Bonhoeffer, Dietrich. *Life Together*. New York: Harper & Row, 1954.
Butterfield, Rosaria Champagne. *The Gospel Comes with a House Key: Practicing Radically Ordinary Hospitality in Our Post-Christian World*. Wheaton, IL: Crossway, 2018.
Calvin, John. *Institutes of the Christian Religion*. Trans. Ford Lewis Battles. Philadelphia, PA: Westminster, 1960.
Carr, Nicholas. *The Shallows: What the Internet Is Doing to Our Brains*. New York: W.W. Norton, 2010.
Como, James. *C. S. Lewis: A Very Short Introduction*. Oxford: Oxford University Press, 2019.
Craig, William Lane. *Reasonable Faith*. Wheaton, IL: Crossway, 2008.
Crouch, Andy. *The Tech-Wise Family: Everyday Steps for Putting Technology in Its Proper Place*. Grand Rapids: Baker Books, 2017.
Dawkins, Richard. *The God Delusion*. New York: Houghton Mifflin, 2006.
Downing, David C. *The Most Reluctant Convert: C. S. Lewis's Journey to Faith*. Downers Grove, IL: IVP Academic, 2002.
Edwards, Bruce L. *A Rhetoric of Belief: C. S. Lewis and the Transformation of Christian Discourse*. Eugene, OR: Wipf & Stock, 2008.
Edwards, Jonathan. "The Christian Pilgrim." In *The Works of Jonathan Edwards*, 2, 244. Edinburgh: Banner of Truth Trust, 1974.
Freud, Sigmund. *The Future of an Illusion*. New York: W.W. Norton & Company, 1927.
———. *Moses and Monotheism*. New York: Vintage Books, 1939.
Hitchens, Christopher. *God Is Not Great: How Religion Poisons Everything*. New York: Twelve, 2007.
Holt-Lunstad, Julianne, et al. "Advancing Social Connection as a Public Health Priority in the United States." *American Psychologist* 72, 6 (2017) 517–30.
Hume, David. *Dialogues Concerning Natural Religion*. Edited by Richard H. Popkin. Indianapolis: Hackett, 1998.

Jacobs, Alan. *The Narnian: The Life and Imagination of C. S. Lewis*. New York: HarperOne, 2008.
Kant, Immanuel. *Religion Within the Bounds of Mere Reason*. Cambridge: Cambridge University Press, 1998.
Keller, Timothy. *The Reason for God: Belief in an Age of Skepticism*. New York: Penguin Books, 2018.
Lewis, C. S. *The Abolition of Man*. New York: HarperOne, 1943.
———. *Collected Letters of C. S. Lewis: Volume 1, Family Letters 1905-1931*. New York: HarperOne, 2004.
———. *Collected Letters of C. S. Lewis: Volume 2, Books, Broadcasts, and the War 1931-1949*. New York: HarperOne, 2004.
———. *God in the Dock: Essays on Theology and Ethics*. Grand Rapids: Eerdmans, 1970.
———. *The Great Divorce*. New York: Macmillan, 1945.
———. *Letters to Malcolm: Chiefly on Prayer*. San Diego: Harvest, 1964.
———. *Mere Christianity*. New York: Touchstone, 1996.
———. *Miracles*. San Francisco: HarperOne, 2001.
———. *Present Concerns: Journalistic Essays*. New York: Harcourt, Brace, & Co., 1986.
———. *The Problem of Pain*. New York: Macmillan, 1940.
———. *Reflections on the Psalms*. New York: Harcourt, Brace & Co., 1958.
———. *The Screwtape Letters*. New York: Macmillan, 1942.
———. *Surprised by Joy: The Shape of My Early Life*. New York: Harcourt, 1955.
———. *The Weight of Glory and Other Addresses*. New York: HarperCollins, 2001.
———. "They Asked for a Paper." In *Is Theology Poetry?* London: Geoffrey Bless, 1962.
MacIntyre, Alasdair. *After Virtue*. Notre Dame, IN: University of Notre Dame Press, 2007.
Marsden, George. *C. S. Lewis's "Mere Christianity": A Biography*. Princeton: Princeton University Press, 2016.
McGrath, Alister E. *C. S. Lewis - A Life: Eccentric Genius, Reluctant Prophet*. Wheaton, IL: Tyndale, 2013.
———. *Mere Apologetics: How to Help Seekers & Skeptics Find Faith*. Grand Rapids: Baker Books, 2012.
Moreland, J.P. *Love Your God with All Your Mind: The Role of Reason in the Life of the Soul*. Colorado Springs, CO: NavPress, 2012.
Nietzsche, Friedrich. *The Gay Science*. New York: Vintage, 1974.
———. *Thus Spoke Zarathustra*. Translated by Walter Kaufmann. New York: Penguin, 1978.
Pascal, Blaise. *Pensées*. Translated by A.J. Krailsheimer. London: Penguin Books, 1995.
Pearcey, Nancy. *Love Thy Body: Answering Hard Questions about Life and Sexuality*. Grand Rapids: Baker Books, 2018.
Peterson, Eugene. *The Pastor: A Memoir*. New York: HarperOne, 2011.
Phillips, Justin. *C. S. Lewis in a Time of War*. New York: HarperOne, 2002.
Plantinga, Alvin. *Where the Conflict Really Lies: Science, Religion, and Naturalism*. New York: Oxford University Press, 2011.
Postman, Neil. *Amusing Ourselves to Death: Public Discourse in the Age of Show Business*. New York: Penguin Books, 1985.
Putnam, Robert D. *Bowling Alone: The Collapse and Revival of American Community*. New York: Simon & Schuster, 2000.
Reppert, Victor. *C. S. Lewis's Dangerous Idea: In Defense of the Argument from Reason*. Downers Grove, IL: IVP Academic, 2003.

BIBLIOGRAPHY

Russell, Bertrand. *Religion and Science*. New York: Oxford University Press, 1935.

———. *Why I Am Not a Christian: And Other Essays on Religion and Related Subjects*. New York: Simon & Schuster, 1957.

Sartre, Jean-Paul. *Existentialism Is a Humanism*. New Haven, CT: Yale University Press, 2007.

Sayer, George. *Jack: A Life of C. S. Lewis*. Wheaton, IL: Crossway, 1994.

Smith, Christian; Denton, Melinda Lundquist. *Soul Searching: The Religious and Spiritual Lives of American Teenagers*. Oxford: Oxford University Press, 2005.

Smith, James K.A. *Desiring the Kingdom*. Grand Rapids: Baker Academic, 2009.

———. *You Are What You Love: The Spiritual Power of Habit*. Grand Rapids: Baker Publishing Group, 2016.

Solomon, Robert C. *Living with Nietzsche: What the Great "Immoralist" Has to Teach Us*. New York: Oxford University Press, 2003.

Taylor, Charles. *A Secular Age*. Cambridge, MA: Harvard University Press, 2007.

Trueman, Carl R. *The Rise and Triumph of the Modern Self*. Wheaton, IL: Crossway, 2020.

Vanhoozer, Kevin J. *Faith Speaking Understanding: Performing the Drama of Doctrine*. Louisville, KY: Westminster John Knox, 2014.

Voltaire. *Philosophical Dictionary*. New York: Basic Books, 1962.

Willard, Dallas. *The Divine Conspiracy*. San Francisco, CA: Harper Collins, 1998.

www.ingramcontent.com/pod-product-compliance
Lightning Source LLC
Chambersburg PA
CBHW071441160426
43195CB00013B/1987